Brown / Trans / Les

Talia Bhatt

author of "Trans/Rad/Fem"

This book is dedicated to my gold and silver, and to every friend who dragged me across the finish line. May the world one day deserve us.

TABLE OF CONTENTS

PRAISE FOR TRANS/RAD/FEM

"Talia Bhatt's incisive prose is a hot knife applied to the soft butter of so much contemporary discourse around transness and feminism. Her unabashed embrace of truly radical elements in a radical feminist tradition that is at this point half a century old gives her perspective a paradoxical freshness at a time when so many conversations on these topics feel like they've reached dead ends." — Susan Stryker, Professor Emerita of Gender and Women's Studies at the Univeristy of Arizona and co-founder of *Trans Studies Quarterly.*

"Talia Bhatt uses a radical feminist framework to make a bold and compelling case that women's and trans people's oppression are deeply intertwined. An important contribution to both trans and feminist theory." — Julia Serano, author of *Whipping Girl.*

"Talia Bhatt's writing is a revelation, a revindication, and a razor-sharp dissection of the ways that patriarchy, Western chauvinism, and transmisogyny have deeply influenced most contemporary approaches to feminism and queer and trans liberation. In crackling prose that encompasses both intellectual clarity and deep feeling, Bhatt draws from both lived experience and academic expertise to clearly illuminate a vision of radical feminism that perceives trans women, trans lesbians, and those forced into "third sex" categories as full human beings rather than political symbols or objects of projection. Bhatt fearlessly and gracefully takes apart many assumptions that have become core to liberal and neoliberal approaches to queer and trans activism, such as the notion of a "gender binary" that must be overturned and the Orientalist fantasy of gender utopian pre-colonial societies - and in doing so, opens up the possibility of liberation work that is rooted in deeper solidarity and greater revolutionary potential. I wish that I could send this book back in time to my younger self - and to all the trans women longing for a clearer reflection of our lives. This is a book that is sure to reshape the discourse on trans femininity, and it stands powerfully alongside the work of thinkers such as Vivian Namaste, Mirha Soleil-Ross, and Julia Serano." — Kai Cheng Thom, author of *Fierce Femmes and Notorious Liars.*

"... like a shot of ice-cold aquavit and a roundhouse kick to the face. Read it." — Sandy Stone, founding scholar of Trans Studies.

"Talia Bhatt's *Trans/Rad/Fem* is a bold, fresh, and unapologetic dissection of how misogyny, lesbophobia, and transmisogyny emerge from the throes of patriarchy. By embracing the best of radical feminist analysis, it sheds a scathing light on the material foundations of patriarchal oppression—and the collective failure to meaningfully undermine them. Acerbic, poetic, and even humorous at times, *Trans/Rad/Fem* is a must-read for anyone in need of an accessible and shrewd overview of gender as a system of policing—and isn't that all of us? Radical feminism has long had a bad rep in leftist circles. Talia Bhatt is well on her way to changing that." — Florence Ashley, author of *Banning Transgender Conversion Practices* and *Gender/Fucking*.

INTRODUCTION
RACE V. GENDER

A few days before I finished this manuscript, a group chat inflicted the existence of Calla Walsh on me.

Walsh is apparently a very young self-described communist who regularly puts out propaganda for regime media outlets such as the Islamic Republic of Iran Broadcasting Corporation. Her opinions can generously be described as "a warped sense of anti-colonialism", in the sense that she seems to uncritically praise and support those nations that are geopolitically opposed to the United States, irrespective of how their governments treat women, queers, ethnic minorities or indeed, communists. (Iran's current leader, in particular, executed many leftist political prisoners in 1988.) Keeping this mind makes the following tweet from Walsh, posted in January 2026, feel very strange to read:

"Sorry but Iran treats women far better than the pedophilic rape cult Western regimes built upon the genocide and mass sex trafficking of women. This shouldn't be controversial, you are just mentally imprisoned."

A comrade with whom I discussed Walsh's niche but outsized prominence in US leftist circles assured me that her views were considered somewhat esoteric even amongst the most eclectic of so-called Third-Worldists, given her startling paucity of nuance and somewhat blatant willingness to be a regime mouthpiece. But that was just the issue. Walsh's tweet did not alarm because it was a self-identified US communist spouting such an alarmingly reductive view of the world in service of a singular ideological fixation. It alarmed me because it was not the first time I'd heard such views from Westerners, including those who consider themselves feminists, queer theorists, decolonial activists, and anti-racists.

Almost as a seeming correction to the jingoism of the early 2000s, a certain slice of those who espouse progressive politics appear to have retreated into a position that rendering any judgment or acknowledging any shortcomings of non-Western societies and cultures is impossible, or at the very least gauche and in all likelihood bigoted. Debates within fields such as anthropology, with a history of racist and colonial consent-manufacturing in their own right, aim to grapple with the question of moral relativism and what it means to discuss other cultures while leaving behind one's (presumptively) Western biases. How should topics such as the marginalization of women and queer people or practices such as FGM and child brides be discussed, especially with an existing history of such subjects being mobilized to construct a hierarchy between an Enlightened West and Primitive Third World?

What if such practices are simply in line with the local values, and passing judgment on them is superimposing a Western and colonial model of values on a non-Western society? Is it not racist and culturally imperialist to insist upon the existence of universal values and systems of morality that are inevitably going to center around Western philosophies and epistemologies? And given that the West is itself far from perfect, should Western scholars not keep a more open mind when

2

ascertaining how harmful certain non-Western beliefs and systems truly are?

You know, mealy-mouthed blathering for those without a backbone.

There's an interesting logic at play here. I've had an actual professor of gender and trans studies tell me on social media that the trans women of my country don't want access to transition care or legal recognition, but rather an end to casteism, capitalism, and colonialism. It's a little magic trick that purports to be 'decolonial', but always by down-playing the importance of feminist struggles and somewhat ironically recentering the primacy of the West and its harms on societies worldwide over any internal struggles or contradictions that may manifest in a complex society with its own demographics and hierarchies to preserve. How dare white feminists claim to care about Muslim women when all they talk about is the hijab? Don't they know that Muslim women care more about an end to worldwide US hegemony?

At the risk of blowing everyone's mind, I humbly suggest: they can want both.

My previous work *Trans/Rad/Fem* is not exactly void of commentary on race, or even on this exact topic. Its largest and most widely-read essay is, after all, on the orientalism of Western academic disciplines with regards to non-Western trans populations. But when I began writing this follow-up, I wanted to make explicit the issue of race, and specifically the issue of how race is now and has historically been mobilized against feminism, as though feminist analysis is simply incapable of adequately accounting for racial hierarchies when discussing patriarchy. As though the widely-popularized but inadequately read canon of Black feminist thought contained within it a proof that feminism is just something white women do to be racist, and really isn't worth anyone's time to take seriously.

I would go as far as to call this a form of anti-intellectualism and *epistemic injustice*—that is, the devaluation of a knowledge-system, namely feminist epistemologies, in service of propping up hegemonic narratives. Because why is it that it's always *feminism* that's too reactionary, too rigid, too fragile and too homogenous and too frivolous to be a worthy pursuit for the colonized and imperialized? Why is it that discourses on race are assumed to contain within them no competing schools, no differing points of view or points of internal contradiction, but the existence of such within feminist disciplines is viewed as an invalidation of the whole subject?

Why, exactly, do people keep assuming that racialized women are too racialized to *be* women? That we are too racialized to be oppressed *as* women?

This book, much like my previous one, is ultimately a book about borders. It is about imaginary boundaries, constructed and treated as too real, by those who are too invested in policing their crossings. It is about feminism, and race, and colonialism, yes, but over and above everything it is about *Nationalism*—about the formation of communities whose interests you are assumed to stand for without question upon being inducted. It about the violence and bloodshed it takes to maintain such lines in the sand, and about asking us all to consider:

What will happen when we refuse to treat these boundaries as real?

1

DEGENDERING AND RACIALIZATION

...or: Do cis women of color "experience transmisogyny"?

PART I: STERILIZATION AND ABORTION

The Jane Collective was an underground organization of feminists operational in Chicago from roughly 1969 to 1973, dedicated to providing women access to safe abortions. At a time when abortion was illegal in most of the United States, reproductive justice remained accessible only to those who could travel to countries where it was legal or available, such as Japan, Mexico, or England. Members of the Jane Collective ended up taking matters into their own hands—quite literally, with several members learning how to perform safe abortions themselves and helping women who couldn't afford an overseas trip.

One of the group's founders was Jody Howard, who had been radicalized by her experiences with the medical industry's regulation of reproductive autonomy. Howard had been diagnosed with Hodgkin's lymphoma during her second pregnancy and had been unable to access treatment during term, as said treatment would have damaged the fetus. This allowed the disease to advance unchecked until she'd given birth, which nearly resulted in her death.

To avoid another pregnancy—one that might actually succeed in killing her—Howard sought and was repeatedly denied tubal ligations from various hospitals until she was able to procure letters from ten different doctors. Though she was eventually able to avail of the procedure, she was told when she woke that she was already pregnant. Howard was then faced with the prospect of securing an abortion, or else braving the very nightmare she had been desperately hoping to avoid.

Fortunately, she was able to do so, by convincing two psychiatrists that she would kill herself if she was unable to get one. This intrusion of the psychiatric establishment into matters of gendered autonomy is already quite illustrative of the logics at play, but more telling is an interesting detail about the hospitals that denied and delayed Howard's voluntary sterilization. Those very same hospitals were, in fact, providing sterilization treatments to women *non-consensually*, a seeming contradiction that is resolved when one considers an important difference between Howard and the sorts of women who have been subject to forced sterilization in the West.

To the state, Judy Howard's gestational capacity was of such paramount importance that she could not be allowed to exercise any agency over it, despite her already being a mother of two. All the while, there were entire classes of women whose gestational capacity was curbed, diminished, denied and destroyed. Treated, in effect, as a threat to be managed, or as offal to discard.

Culling the children, the *future* of 'undesirables', has always been core to the project of Nation-building, after all.

PART II: BINARY WOMANHOOD

Readers familiar with radical transfeminism understand how *degendering* is a core component of *transmisogyny*. Trans women are most frequently denied womanhood on the basis of our lack of *gestational capacity*, that characteristic that is, under patriarchal society, indelibly and inseparably associated with the class 'woman'. The similarities between how trans women and infertile cis women are treated—which includes but is not limited to elevated rates of sexual violence, degradation as 'defective' or 'barren' women, and third-sexing out of gendered categorization entirely—are usually ignored to promulgate this rhetorical violence and maintain cissexist notions of 'natural', immutable and dichotomous sex.

From this, it is easy to infer that while 'woman' is a term easily defined by its relationship to reproduction and sexed autonomy under the heterosexual regime, it self-evidently remains internally heterogeneous. Most patriarchal societies quite overtly maintain a distinction between women of the hegemonic demographic, who are demarcated as reproductive resources to be parcelled out within the private, domestic sphere, and "the rest": women who are, to put it bluntly, placed on a lower 'tier'. "The kind you don't take home to mama."

Transmisogyny is *far* from the only force that destabilizes a woman's relationship to the patriarchal bargain. Race, disability, and sexuality immediately come to mind (non-exhaustively) as 'mitigating factors' that represent a form of downward mobility in the gendered hierarchy,

7

intensifying the misogyny women face through avenues of sexual exploitation or corrective, reclamatory violence.

Given that race is a social technology that encodes certain relationships to *citizenship*, *nationality*, *ancestry*, and/or *colonization*, it is trivial to understand how it can be deployed as a tool of degendering. When it comes to ranking reproductive resources, or what eugenicists have actually referred to as *breeding stock*, racialization *devalues* womanhood, rendering a woman 'less fit' for exploitation within the domicile, less able to (re)produce the Nation's ideal Citizen, its vaunted and valorized (racial) hegemony. Racialized women are thus frequently *sexualized*, while commensurately being just as frequently excluded from the Nation's 'ideal' pool of broodmares.

If one is tempted at this juncture to try and understand the 'ranking' of various categories of woman, a future essay will explicate on why that is a futile endeavor. For now, it is sufficient to understand that such social 'rankings' are always highly *contextual*, and that for the topic at hand, we only need to know that women, by and large, experience a fairly *binary* categorization: those valued for their gestational capacity, and *everyone else*.

That is, in fact, the best way to understand how third-sexing functions.

PART III: 'MASCULINIZED'

This degendering that racialized women are subject to is usually referred to, in the common parlance, as women of color being 'masculinized'. The term fails to communicate the actual mechanisms at play on several levels, which we'll examine here.

The first issue is the concept of 'masculinity' itself, a characteristic that those who live under patriarchal regimes intuitively understand but struggle to put into words, especially when engaging with feminist discourses. Queer theorist Jack Halberstam defines 'masculinity' in the introduction to his book *Female Masculinity* as "I don't know, vibes" (paraphrased—but barely). Most people have a tendency to hem and haw and pretend that 'masculinity' is some nebulous, arbitrary collection of positive attributes such as "strength" and "leadership", and stop replying when asked why feminine women cannot embody them.

When peeling back the charade and speaking honestly about patriarchal gendering, however, it is easy to understand masculinity as simply the set of positive attributes that men are both expected to and assumed to embody, characterizing them as possessing agency, as free from patriarchal gendering. It is thus a concept defined entirely through antithesis, antagonism, and mutual exclusivity with the feminine, the womanly, the *meek*. *Strong, masculine, virile, intellectual* men are held up in contrast to *weak, effeminate, vapid,* and *penetrable* women. Masculinity and femininity are therefore simply social encodings for dichotomous sexed roles, ones that have varied across time and culture. Julia Serano, in *Whipping Girl*, has dubbed this 'oppositional sexism', and those familiar with Christian patriarchy may recognize the concept as *complementarianism*.

Keeping this in mind, we can now recognize how dubbing racialized degendering as 'masculinization' is somewhat logically and linguistically incoherent. For even speakers who talk around the social understanding of masculinity know that masculine attributes are regarded as inherently *positive*, as conveying notions of greater agency, responsibility, or capacity as a human being under patriarchy. Even when 'negative' aspects of masculinity are interrogated, such as men's violence being enabled or excused by their legal and sociocultural contexts, that capacity for gendered violence is not regarded as a core, defining aspect of masculinity, but as "toxic" masculinity, as an aberration from a noble ideal that cannot fail, but only *be* failed.

Racialized women are thus hardly being 'masculinized' when degendered. They are not being regarded with more respect or afforded more dignity and agency, and are in fact being constructed as *less* human, *marked* as acceptable targets of brutalization and sexual violence without repercussion. (We would do well to remember, as well, that *masculinity* renders men as the *perpetrators* and not targets of sexual violence, and that men who are subject to such violence themselves are invariably *unmanned, effeminized, emasculated*—degendered in their own right.) The purpose of this dehumanization is certainly homoousian with transmisogyny, but remains distinct in important ways.

To illustrate this, we ought to consider the recent case of Olympic boxer Imane Khelif. Khelif found herself a prominent target of the global trans panic, inadvertently uniting technofeudalists, wizard kidlit authors, and reactionary wingnuts into calling for her disqualification under the guise of "protecting women's sports". As Serano observed in her essay *Why Does "Transvestigation" Happen?*, the rhetoric that is frequently deployed against transfem athletes was used to question Khelif's womanhood, to dub her a "secret" man covertly "invading" women's spaces—in short, instrumentalizing transmisogynistic tropes to degender and vilify her.

Surface-level understandings of this phenomenon would seem to lend credence to the idea that Khelif was 'masculinized'—she was, after all, "called a man"—and also 'subjected to transmisogyny', on account of being treated "like a trans woman". An analysis that runs into issues when considering important distinctions between Imane Khelif and

10

transfem athletes, such as *the complete absence of any transfem athletes competing at the 2024 Olympics.*

Khelif, in essence, had access to an easy defense that a hypothetical trans woman athlete would not have been able to utilize: she could simply point out that the statements made about her sex were not true. Popular defenses of her place at the Olympics did not, ultimately, rest upon affirmations of trans women's place in women's sports, but merely pointed out that she was being lied about and had as much a right to participate as any *female* athlete. It was simply the case that Khelif was cast in the role of "woman to degender and vilify" because the extant global transmisogynistic panic had entirely succeeded in keeping trans women out of the Olympics.

Further, women of color are no more 'treated as men' than trans women are when we are maliciously degendered. Here is yet another case of inflammatory rhetoric and reactionary invective being taken entirely at face value rather than understood for its rhetorical purpose. Though third-sexing and degendering are mechanisms that patriarchal reactionaries understand and deploy intuitively, their schema of sex as dichotomous only allows them to call their targets "men" when attempting to exclude someone from the category "woman". (Even as misogynists fully understand the purpose of gender as a social disciplining tool, they must safeguard the fiction of 'immutable', 'binary' sex, leaving a not-woman or a failed-woman to be called a perverse, violent man.) As noted, this is not 'masculinization', the elevation to the social role of 'man', but rather *dehumanization, bestialization, brutification*—the construction of a target as a brutish, primitive, animalistic threat to 'real women' that can and indeed must be *put down*. While the patriarchy's 'protectionism' over women-as-a-resource is largely a fiction—reproductive assets are claimed, jealously guarded, and exploited, not 'protected'—the purpose of racialized degendering is to exclude women of color from even that flimsy heterosexual contract and leave them only fit for brutalization and/or violent consumption.

Transmisogynistic rhetoric is only the latest tool in the racist reactionary's belt, one that is used to promulgate a long history of racialized degendering. Women of color, lesbians, and women of various other identities have long been opportunistically degendered and expelled from the 'upper echelon' of womanhood down to its third-sexed wastes, *even when people know full well their target is not a man*. One of the first women to fail a chromosomal "sex test" was Ewa Kłobukowska in 1967, a Polish Olympic athlete whose records were stripped from her following this failure, and yet not restored when she gave birth to a child in 1968. In a similar vein, when non-white women are publicly degendered and libeled falsely as violent brutes, the truth of their sex is hardly ever the point. The point is *humiliation*, to *put them in their place* for having overreached, for daring to be present amidst 'their betters' at all.

Khelif's case in particular is incomplete without accounting for her race, and for the role organized sports (and their organizing bodies) have played in upholding the ideology of essentialized sexed differences *and* regimes of racial and national superiority. It is thus not at all a coincidence that the non-transfem athletes whose reputations and records have been consistently harmed by transmisogynistic policies are largely racialized and intersex.

Interpersonally, racialized degendering functions as a means of designating a target for *both* racialized and sexed violence. A racialized woman is degendered not due to an authentic confusion about her gender, but to eject her from the category 'woman'—patriarchally understood as lacking in agency, desire, or autonomous capacity—and regard her as a brutified, bestialized *threat*. Contrasted against hegemonic womanhood, assailants are provided a ready casus belli, their violence against her authorized and justified as the necessary defense of patriarchal property against the external Other. Her body, so marked, becomes an acceptable site of violence. A, for any who oppose her are acting in self-preservation, while any attempt she makes to preserve herself are interpreted as clear and overt signs of aggressive intent.

That, ultimately, was the sin Imane Khelif was made to pay for. No one who participated in her public humiliation had any concrete reason to doubt her sex. They did have a reason to want to punish her for trouncing a white opponent, though, and relished the opportunity to remind her of her station.

Concurrent regimes of violence, after all, tend to *build upon each other*, to intensify mutually reinforcing structures that most acutely harm those who exist at their *intersections*. Yet, despite the intersection of race and sex being one of the most-studied, the ways in which racialization deploys *gendering* is rather neglected. (Trans)misogyny is a tried-and-true method of *degradation* and *dehumanization*, and the racialized regimes we labor under are also patriarchal ones. To say that racialized women experience *transmisogyny* rather than *degendering* is to discount how racialization already destabilizes gendering in service of the National project.

Of course, we must also state the obvious and particularly galling conclusion of asserting that racialized cis women "experience transmisogyny": it erases *trans women of color* from the conversation entirely by collapsing the specificities of our linked but distinct oppressions together. It is not true that trans women of color and cis women of color are treated identically in multiracial, locally white-hegemonic societies, and when we consider societies that are *not* locally white-hegemonic, such as those in the third world, the claim that cis and trans women are treated identically therein is revealed to be *utterly absurd*, as is the usual result of ignoring an important and relevant intersection.

PART IV: NATALISM

In conflating transmisogyny with racialized degendering, we do not simply elide the intersection of the two, but also rob ourselves of the insight that comes from examining the underlying impetus animating both. The reason the treatment of racialized women often mirrors that of trans women writ large is that both classes of women are *devalued* similarly, as inadequate or outright detrimental to the Nation's reproductive ambitions. The function of patriarchy is to instantiate heterosexuality, to manage the sexual chattel and reproductive stock through which its segregated labor pools are both organized and maintained. Additional ideological investments such as the USian settler-colonial order, the Indian varna system, or state religions the world over further bifurcate citizen from underclass, providing the masses with anti-materialist incentives to "buy-in" and identify with their rulers over their fellow exploited humans.

Through the *naturalization* of these caste systems as 'biological fact', their social and ideological character is obscured and reduced to a matter of individual identity. Manhood, whiteness, and similar mantles of social dominance become obfuscated as innate qualities, and the mechanisms of regulation and enforcement that define and dictate membership are invisiblized by the prevailing epistemic orthodoxy.

Social dominance, then, is best understood in terms of managing affinity, fealty, affiliation, *investment* in the prevailing social order. Those who are able to access and leverage any scraps of power will often do so eagerly and unthinkingly, disincentivized as they are to examine the basis of their own privileging. Even those who are not positioned to derive the most benefits still usually find compliance to be more frictionless than questioning authority and cultural wisdom. Many, if not most, accede to the bargains they are provided, choosing to ameliorate their own exploitation and suffering by participating in others', or even by merely reinforcing the constructed boundary between their identity and the assigned identities of those more abject, more reviled.

Recall, once more, the most common defenses of Imane Khelif. Instead of challenging the transmisogynistic precepts that would declare a trans woman's participation illegitimate or as a threat to "actual women", the majority of Khelif's defenders opted to engage in *identitarian distancing*, with the appeal that she did not deserve the transmisogynistic invalidation that a hypothetical transfeminine athlete could not demand exemption from. Yes, it is entirely true that the racist degendering and harassment Khelif experienced could highlight points of solidarity between two similarly oppressed classes of women, but that wasn't what happened. Instead, trans women's vilification was declared as misplaced and tragic when it spilled over to others, resulting in appeals to minimize the collateral damage.

Disentangling these threads is a concerted effort in unravelling imprecise language and the varying degrees of epistemic violence to which that all marginalized classes are subject to. While it would bring me nothing but joy to see racialized cis women—among whom I count some of my dearest friends and allies—collectively identify more with the trans women who are degendered alongside them and the transmisogyny we face, the disappointments of material reality remain, and racialized cis women are often just as invested in cisness as their white counterparts. If they can reinforce the difference between themselves and trans women, if they can secure their own place within woman-hood—however abject or tenuous—by denying us ours, it remains true that many, if not most, will do just that.

Not all the transfems are white, and not all the racialized women are cis, leaving those of us betwixt with no choice but to be brave, given how frequently we are forgotten, abandoned, and ... alone. Women like me must mind both meanings of 'passing', requiring us to make peace with how, no matter how indistinguishable we are from racialized cis women, our gender is still always subject to challenge under a white hegemony.

Finally, the bitterest pill remains the most evident one. Because for all her experience with degendering, all the experiences that should give her insight into the indignities of racialization, the white trans woman is often unable to resist the temptation of partaking in *racialized trans-misogyny*, lured in by the siren song of being enabled to implement identitarian distance herself, against a woman placed below even her. Despite being given every chance to embrace sameness over difference, the chance to prove her womanhood against the degendering of those easily cast as rapacious, alien, animalistic predators tends to be reward enough.

I must repeat: the similarities between the cis and trans women of a race-class abound, including whom they are allowed to enact violence against, and how they leverage their access to patriarchal protectionism.

Which stands conclusively as the grandest irony of all. Yes, even here, in the unholiest of unholies, I am offal amidst offal, a tranny amidst trannies. We're all trans, and I'm still brown—this is a lesson I've learned all too well. What makes the irony rich is that my place here is so readily reinforced by those who can no more avail of the patriarchal bargain than I can, who will in the final calculus be looked upon no more favorably than a third-sexed, degendered *thing* from the wrong Nation. Dworkin noted astutely in *The Coming Gynocide* that a society which apportions women value based on fertility will also discard them the moment they prove fallow, that *longevity* and *security* are the commodities patriarchy withholds from us most of all. One day, you will be offal too, and serving me up before that day comes will not prevent its arrival, or even meaningfully delay it.

Heed or ignore that warning at your own peril. Under the current regimes, our fates are entwined, and our ignominious end inevitable, unless ...

Unless.

2
INTERSECTIONAL ANTIFEMINISM, OR: WHAT IS A WHITE FEMINIST, ANYWAY?

INTRODUCTION: WHITE/RAD/FEM

There is a specter haunting feminism: insubstantial, ghostly pale, and —so goes the charge—one highly resistant to exorcism. Too long has this ruling-class pastime, borne of diabolically idle minds and idler spirits, threatened to undermine the solidarity of *true, revolutionary* movements, seeking to sow the seeds of separatism such that sexed solipsism supersedes syncretic struggle! Splitting sister from brother, wife from husband, and maiden from suitor, the forked-tongued feminist flits about in the garb of a noble liberator, pouring her *racist, bourgeois,* and *essentialist* poison into any unwitting, innocent ear she's lent, corrupting the minds of young women with her preposterous ideas.

For the feminist is *always* white, affluent, and biologically-deterministic, an individual that does not *truly* suffer in any meaningful way, yet consistently and exuberantly cites her sex to obfuscate her privileges, exaggerate her marginalization, and deny her capacity to harm. In doing so she aims to engender a false consciousness, concocting an ersatz sorority between herself and the *actually oppressed* women whose subjugation she benefits from, and is invested in perpetuating.

Of course, women *are* actually oppressed—no one denies that—but marginalized women (a category mutually exclusive with the feminist, of course) have *real* actual oppression to combat, unlike the silly sex-antagonism that feminists concern themselves with. The racialized woman aspires to the dismantling of white supremacy, the proletarian woman an end to capitalist hegemony, and the colonized woman longs for the emancipation of all her people! Meanwhile, feminists—being the ultimate beneficiaries of all these systems of exploitation—wish for marginalized women to quarrel endlessly with men of their own class and race and nation. Marginalized women are thus enticed to *ally with their oppressors*— that is, feminists. Their fellow men, naturally, have always taken their concerns seriously—which is to say, guided them to focus on the issues that *affect them all*, rather than quibble over frivolities such as domestic confinement and reproductive labor and sexual violence, which affect only *some* of them—impossible to tell which of them, even.

Unlike the feminist, the actually oppressed marginalized woman understands her place in the movement. She nobly supports her comrades, magnanimously upholds the common banner, and places the collective's concerns above her own with divinely-feminine grace. She is a mother to the movement—and wife and lover and scullery-maid, too—happy in her place and overjoyed to do the thankless, joyless, uncompensated, unrecognized, and uncredited work that must be done.

Could there theoretically be feminists that are not manipulative, deceitful mouthpieces of the ruling-classes? Perhaps someday, there may yet be. Today, however, there is no such thing as a non-white, non-Western, non-rich, non-cis, non-ugly feminist, as surely as there does not exist a non-misandrist lesbian. Do not fall for their propaganda, comrades, and do not shirk your duty to the cause by presuming that your gender matters more than any other identity through which men can lay claim to you. Do not forget who your true enemy is: *other women*.

PART ONE: THE THREE INTERSECTIONALITIES

In 1989, legal theorist and feminist Kimberlé Crenshaw published *Demarginalizing the intersection of race and sex*, establishing the most groundbreaking social theory that no one seems to have read. Many, many people want to give the impression that they have read it, however, so that they may position themselves as experts on the topic to others who have read even less. The motivations for this co-optation vary, but can be organized into three broad camps: conservative 'intellectual', liberal commentator, and leftist iconoclast.

For the conservative, the motive is straightforward epistemic vandalism, a twisting and redefinition of a term to obfuscate its actual purpose and undermine progressive social movements. The word "woke" and the field of "critical race theory"—ironically, another school where Crenshaw is a towering figure—are examples of such discursive defacing (and it is no accident that every phrase under consideration here stems from Black activism and scholarship). In a 2019 Vox article entitled hilariously as the "Intersectionality Wars", conservative 'intellectuals' no less illustrious than Ben Shapiro himself describe intersectionality as a "new caste system", intended to place cis, straight, white men "at the bottom".

While the inadvertent admission that there must have existed an *old* caste system for intersectionality to supplant is revealing, the blatant dishonesty of the statements border on parodic. Social theories cannot with a single stroke undo centuries of disenfranchisement, exploitation, and hollowing-out, any more than one can get Ben Shapiro to quit yapping for just two minutes. Even without an understanding of intersectionality, it should be obvious that this perceived epistemic threat—this idea that the most dominant voices will somehow be drowned out and be left at the mercy of the most silenced—is nothing but yet another reactionary persecution fantasy, an attempt to cast any attempts at elucidating the plight of the marginalized as violence against not the hegemony, but those of the hegemonic demographic.

It is a strategy that will continue to be deployed for as long as it remains effective.

Meanwhile, the liberal is eager to take up the mantle of intersectionality, even if she is somewhat fuzzy on what exactly taking that mantle up entails. So eager and enthusiastic is she, in fact, that she insists on having *always* championed it, claiming that her feminism and antiracism and general social project has *always* been intersectional! Never mind the why and when of intersectionality's popularization, because even when she wasn't using the *word*, the *intent* was always there. After all, look at how *lucrative*—that is to say, *generalizable*—the concept is! Any assertion can spawn a critique to a response to a subheading, by highlighting just how *lacking in intersectionality* it is. Does your paper or project account for race *and* sex *and* ability *and* sexuality *and* affluence *and* immigrant status? It does? Well, what about religion, caste, bilinguality, education level, height, geographic location, and weather on Tuesdays? Keep 'em coming—there's grants to secure!

After all, was that not intersectionality's greatest innovation—the construction of tier lists and rankings of oppressed identities? Forget regimes and the hierarchies they instantiate! Instead, draw up your character sheet, where each axis of marginalization represents a "debuff" or "deviation" from the state of "default human", while listing every "privilege" that you must acknowledge and repent for. This is surely the approach that Crenshaw intended and certainly not something she critiqued the very legal system for in her original paper! By tallying these oppression points up, we can determine who has the most epistemic authority to speak on *any* and *every* topic, on account of being The Most Intersectional. Finally, the kyriarchy is over.

Of course, anyone with that high a rank in Intersectionality surely couldn't also have the *most* right to speak. If they have a platform, can speak English, or are just too *articulate*—why, those are all *privileges* that bar them from being the most intersectional person in the room! Indeed, anyone can have internalized misogyny or racism or ableism or any other kind of bigotry, and saying the wrong things or otherwise challenging the material roots of systems of oppression proves that they likely are too *academic, eloquent,* and frankly not intersectional *enough*! Intersectionality tells us, after all, that *men* are oppressed too, that *men of color* cannot uphold patriarchy because white supremacy disempowers them—never mind what they do in order to secure that lost masculinity! bell hooks who? Anyway, it would probably be best if someone more *qualified* to speak on intersectional matters spoke up on behalf of the Actual Most Intersectional and Oppressed Person, who of course is too oppressed to even be present in the room.

That was the brilliant insight that Ben Shapiro missed—no one can wield intersectionality as a cudgel quite like white people can.

However, all this talk of intersectionality in the mainstream has proven that it has already been recuperated by the bourgeois academy and liberal establishment, irrespective of whether or not its tenets are being accurately understood or represented. The leftist, therefore, remains unmoved by all these silly revisionist distractions, all these identitarian and idealist social constructs that serve only to clutter up Marx —I mean, Mao—or Lenin, or perhaps Kropotkin, if you're not a filthy statist? Look, it's polluting the purity of *someone's* theory, and we'll figure out exactly whose, roughly around the time the state withers away, so long as we stick to the five-year plans.

In the meantime, we cannot let identity politics compromise solidarity by creating false antagonisms where none exist among the *working class*, a historically homogenous entity with no internal contradictions whatsoever. Myopic focus on oppressor/oppressed dichotomies hinder us from recognizing that our true enemy remains the capitalist class, and we only need to disseminate the Perfectly Persuasive and True Science of Socialism to snap literally anyone out of their identification with bourgeois ideologies, so long as they are proletarian! No proletarian has ever materially benefited from or remained invested in the oppression of another proletarian, of course, and no ruling-class worth its salt has ever sown divisions among the masses that prove to be more enduring and persuasive than simple material interest!

Oh, except intersectionality. That one's definitely a CIA plot, which I can prove with this image of Crenshaw standing next to Hillary Clinton.

In any case, we can all agree on one thing—we all know what intersectionality is, understand it perfectly, and don't talk about it in a manner that makes me want to claw my own face off.

PART TWO: JUST READ THE DAMN PAPER

So, after all of that, what *is* intersectionality, really? What truth about interlocking systems of oppression does it reveal, and how precisely can we incorporate it in analyses of overlapping identities and marginalizations?

Demarginalizing the intersection of race and sex walks the reader through three specific cases to illustrate the multidimensionality of Black women's experiences, in the context of antidiscrimination law. Crenshaw shows us how courts are happy to apply inconsistent and indeed contradictory logics in service not of American jurisprudence, but American reaction, the American regime of racialization and patriarchy and settler-colonial logics.

In *DeGraffenreid v General Motors*, the district court rejected the plaintiffs' attempt to bring a suit alleging employment discrimination against Black women. Despite the fact that General Motors did not hire a single Black woman prior to 1964, and all Black women hired after 1970 were deprived of their jobs in a seniority-based layoff, the suit was rejected on the grounds that GM did hire white women (therefore, could not be accused of sex discrimination) and also hired Black men (which meant there was no evidence of race discrimination).

Most gallingly, the court stated that the plaintiffs "should not be allowed to combine statutory remedies to create a new 'super remedy'". The audacity of this assertion is best illustrated by the court's *own admission* that Black women could be discriminated against on the basis of race *or* sex, even as it alleged that it was somehow absurd for them to claim *both*. There is a perfect awareness here that Black women can be injured in ways that either white women or Black men cannot be, but the specter of a "super-protected" class is invoked to deny them *any* relief at all.

After all, imagine if there was a class of person accorded special privileges in the US-American legal system—how out of the ordinary that would be!

This is a conclusion that stands in stark contrast to the decisions examined in the two following cases, one a case of sex discrimination and the other a case of race discrimination. In *DeGraffenreid*, it was found that Black women were similar enough to white women and Black men that discrimination against them, specifically, could not be established in the absence of discrimination against either preceding class. However, *Moore v Hughes Helicopter, Inc* and *Payne v Travenol* both concluded that Black women were *too different* from either white women or Black men to be the representative plaintiffs in cases of either sex or race discrimination!

Taken together, we can observe how Black women are denied relief based on their alleged *sameness* or *difference* to other demographics. Either they are too similar to (for example) other unharmed women to establish any particular harms against them on the basis of sex, or they are too distinct from other women to be considered truly representative of the wider category. Crenshaw, here, highlights how these opportunistic logics are oriented not around legal or logical consistency, but rather are the thinnest rationalizations available to reinforce Black women's particular state of marginality. Further, they illustrate a dilemma that Black women are faced with both legally and socially, in courtrooms and activism and social movements: to 'declare allegiance' to their race or their sex, to claim injury as women or as Black people, but never both.

Black women, and racialized women more generally, have the particularized harms they face as both women *and* racialized people invisi-bilized, an epistemic injustice that is rooted in denying how the multi-plicity of their marginalization intensifies their precarity and the violences they face.

Crenshaw's firm, uncompromising assertion is this: *we shouldn't have to choose.* We shouldn't have to subdivide aspects of our identity to decide which is the 'most' injured, the 'most' relevant to the current situation, because at no point are we ever *just* women, or *just* racialized, or even *just* lesbians, disabled, working-class, Jewish, etc. Every injury we sustain is impacted by the multiplicity of our identities and experi-ences because that is how we exist in the world—not as an assemblage of discrete identities but as singular, *whole* people, whose marginaliza-tion both resembles the bigotry faced by those less-marginalized, and is also uniquely intensified by the gestalt of our marginalizations.

Intersectionality, then, is a revolutionary theory that asks us to reckon with the reality of the multiply-marginalized woman on *her* terms, rather than picking and choosing the parts of her that are most useful or convenient to us. It uncompromisingly asserts that in order to effectively advocate for anyone, we must ensure that we are advocating for and listening to the most marginalized amongst us (who is usually a woman), instead of aiding in her epistemic burial.

And ever since its publication, no one has forgiven Crenshaw for making that point.

INTERLUDE: NO INTERSECTIONALITY FOR WOMEN

If you understand intersectionality, its repeated diminishment and co-optation to serve the ends of anyone *but* the most-marginalized is truly hysteria-inducing to witness. Anecdotal though my experiences are, time and time again every feminist I know, whether white or not, whether trans or not, whether queer or not, has related the same story that I do: of being called "white feminist", "TERFy", or *non-intersectional* for stating that male-supremacy animates patriarchy, or otherwise stating that men exploit women.

Dominance feminism in particular—which is the central radical feminist assertion of patriarchal society being founded upon the subjugation of women-as-a-class, by men-as-a-class—is frequently decried as 'essentialist', and consequently as 'incompatible' with intersectionality. Of the two charges levied against it, the first tends to be that regarding all women as a unified demographic with shared class interests elides the many contradictions that exist amongst women: principally race, but also class, ability, sexuality, and more. As an example, implying that women of color share interests with white women is an anti-intersectional act—supposedly—that erases how white women benefit from their racial privileges at the expense of women of color.

Sealing the deal, the second charge against dominance feminism is that it papers over the cases where *women* are privileged over *men*, once more principally deploying race to make the argument. To deny that affluent white women oppress working-class Black men, as dominance feminism—supposedly—does, is to deny a fundamental social reality of US-American society, to instrumentalize sex for reactionary purposes and perpetuate harmful stereotypes of "male threat" against men of color that have been used to justify violence and carceralism against them since the very inception of the United States.

(Astute readers, at this point, might be arching their brows and itching to ask questions, such as "Wait, what about working-class Black women? What about patriarchal societies that aren't or precede the

United States?" That is not important right now. We are demonstrating why feminism is bad.)

By demonstrating these deficiencies, we have conclusively proved that dominance feminism is a bad theory: it fails to grapple with *nuanced* analyses that illustrate why women of color do not share gendered interests with white women, and *intersectional* analyses that account for racialized men. (Those who might be asking how 'racialized man' is an intersectional identity—what other marginalization is their racialization intersecting with, in this example?—are surely non-intersectional in their own right.) We therefore cannot trust any feminist theory that insists that *all men* oppress *all women*, as dominance and radical feminisms obviously(?) do. To do so would be to reify the oppressive logics being neglected to advance a sex-essentialist agenda, and would be colonial and white-supremacist and transphobic and bourgeois and worse!

Truly, no more infallibly compelling argument has ever been made.

I must confess that when I began to conceptualize this essay, I had consigned myself to arguing my case on largely autoethnographic merits, to forefront personal experience and brace for the eventual charges that I was exaggerating a rare reactionary tendency, or generalizing too much from my own accounts. Imagine my delight, then, when I came across a 2010 paper that not only points to these discursive tendencies in both academic and activist settings, but also argues vehemently that this is a misuse of intersectionality theory. The author definitively states that the alleged incompatibility between dominance feminist paradigms and intersectionality is not merely exaggerated, but outright incorrect, and places an undue, unfair burden on feminist theories that other social paradigms, such as antiracism, are not expected to answer for. That—I dare infer—the very charge of 'essentialism' is being misapplied for grotesquely antifeminist ends!

Strong claims, all. Hopefully, whoever made them can back up the assertion of understanding intersectionality better than most others, even many academics!

PART THREE: THAT'S NOT WHAT 'ESSENTIALISM' MEANS

I am of course referring to the 2010 paper, *Close Encounters of Three Kinds: On Teaching Dominance Feminism and Intersectionality,* authored by Kimberlé Crenshaw. In it, Crenshaw argues for the saliency of intersectionality as a *feminist* theory, one entirely compatible with the social-constructivist radical feminism of Catherine MacKinnon.

"Listeners often register surprise that MacKinnon would occupy any constructive space in the conceptual universe of intersectionality. I sometimes push the envelope even further by suggesting that her controversial essay *From Practice to Theory, or What Is a White Woman Anyway?* is among my favorite MacKinnon essays to teach."

Here, Crenshaw takes us through three 'encounters' with MacKinnon. Her appreciation and enthusiasm for MacKinnon's contributions to both legal theory and feminism is infectious, and her candid discussion of how this radical feminism has influenced and intersected with her own work is, ultimately, unsurprising. We are told how *Demarginalizing* touches upon MacKinnon's critiques of feminist paradigms that advocate women's equality on the basis of our *sameness* to men, set against arguments that emphasize women's *difference*.

"MacKinnon argued persuasively that sameness and difference were merely different sides of the same coin."

In both cases, "men are the standard", the default by which all other 'deviations' in one's humanity is judged. Where MacKinnon asks why women must hew to a standard set by men, why our humanity is contingent on that which men find worthy of recognition, Crenshaw reiterates the question for the case of Black female plaintiffs. Why must they be judged based on how similar they are to Black men or white women, and *why*—Crenshaw notes pointedly—do any differences preclude Black women from representing *all* women?

For this is one of the more insidious applications of intersectionality, which has been scrutinized and used to call the whole theory into question, but happens to be a practice that Crenshaw has critiques of too: the siloing—the *segregation,* even—of Black women's concerns into their own box that do not meaningfully overlap with that of other women. That Black women face unique issues does not mean their interests are wholly distinct from that of less-marginalized women, merely that they are *more vulnerable*, and require *unique considerations* that are frequently overlooked. Intersectionality is an argument for *forefronting* the most-marginalized, not regarding them as wholly distinct from groups they do in fact share interests with. Notably, there is less separatism when it comes to discussing Black people's interests broadly in antiracist discourses, but it is absolutely rampant in feminist discussions *and* criticisms of feminism.

Interestingly, *What is a White Woman Anyway?* shares and expresses this concern:

"There is nothing biologically necessary about rape, as Mechelle Vinson made abundantly clear when she sued for rape as unequal treatment on the basis of sex. And, as Lillian Garland saw, and made everyone else see, it is the way society punishes women for reproduction that creates women's problems with reproduction, not reproduction itself. **Both women are Black. This only supports my suspicion that if a theory is not true of, and does not work for, women of color, it is not really true of, and will not work for, any women, and that it is not really about gender at all.** The theory of the practice of Mechelle Vinson and Lillian Garland, because it is about the experience of Black women, is what gender is about." [Emphasis mine.]

Catherine MacKinnon, it would seem, has read the damn paper.

Another way in which MacKinnon's work enhances rather than detracts from the thesis in *Demarginalizing* is seen in an observation she makes about reverse-discrimination suits brought by white men in affirmative action cases. It is obvious here that white men cannot represent all men, or all white people, because non-white men and white women alike benefit from affirmative action programs. Nevertheless, their 'compound reverse-discrimination' claims are not merely humored by courts, but are not even identified as grievances specific to *white men*, or cast as an attempt to form a "super-protected" class combining statutory remedies! Preferential treatment, it would seem, only causes a doctrinal crisis when anyone other than white men stand to benefit.

So far, it is expectedly difficult to refute any of Crenshaw's points. Which makes her 'final encounter' with MacKinnon all the more mystifying—the spectral, 'virtual' MacKinnon conjured by the students in her own classes, bearing little resemblance to the real article. Crenshaw's palpable frustration in this section only rivals her writings on *DeGraffenreid*, as she expresses her bafflement at bright, socially-engaged, activist-minded youths who are highly familiar with intersectionality theory, and yet express such disdain for dominance feminism.

"Whether the conversation is marked by the notion of waves (as in second wave, third, etc.) or by temporal references that modify the brand of feminism at issue (post-feminist, neo feminists, or something else), there are numerous indicators that suggest a certain distancing from what is perceived to be **a crude and unappealing feminism**. This distancing has been the subject of analysis and debate for some time, but the particular version of it that emerges most forcefully in my Intersectionalities course wraps its logics either implicitly or explicitly around the primacy of race. This relatively traditional strain of argument frames feminism as a white woman's thing while certain male-centric ideologies about racism continue to win the allegiance of many of my progressive students. This stance rarely involves an explicit rejection of feminism per se, but instead a race-centered critique that repudiates white feminism as an embodiment of racism and hierarchy. Inevitably, MacKinnon's iconic status in legal discourse places her at the epicenter of this frame." [Emphasis mine.]

What perturbs Crenshaw the most is the inconsistency displayed by students who are quick to call 'essentialism' in feminist discussions, yet see little issue with the repeated centering of male perspectives, male leadership, and indeed male suffering when discussing anti-racist or decolonial movements. Apparently, race presents an insurmountable barrier that the category 'woman' can in no way supersede, while racialization is allegedly homogenizing enough to create no meaningful distinctions between the experiences of men and women (and sexual minorities). Her attempts to highlight the contradiction in allowing for this kind of essentialism in one arena but not another are met with truly stupefying rationalizations: that a greater degree of *intimacy* between men and women of the same racial class "creates more empathy" within this group, that men of color advocate for the concerns of women of color better than white feminists do, or that race is simply a more "impactful" marginalization than sex in one's life.

While I could perhaps detail how I've rarely seen men of my race advocate for women of my race in a manner that does not reinforce a sexual property relation between us or otherwise infringe upon their inalienable right to beat us to death without repercussion, there is a correct answer to the conundrum of whether race or sex deserves greater consideration when weighing up how one is marginalized. I present this as an exercise to the reader as well: before peeking ahead, please answer whether you think women of color like me ought to be more concerned with racialization or patriarchy.

The answer, of course, is: *why the fuck are you making that comparison in the first place, you waste of tuition?* Did you not read the damn paper? Classrooms are a place for learning, yes, but falling back on this oppression arithmetic in a class *literally taught by Crenshaw* should be grounds for immediate ejection, surely.

These students' critiques of MacKinnon's essay, when exposed to it, also merit a similar scorn. Despite quite clearly stating the importance of accounting for the most marginalized women, several of Crenshaw's students have alleged that *What is a White Woman Anyway?* is itself a "white feminist" screed through which MacKinnon is somehow reinscribing the primacy of the white woman as the central subject of feminism!

Columbia Law, in spite of its illustrious faculty, is clearly not all it's cracked up to be.

Here, the story of Elaine Brown (who chaired the Black Panther Party from 1974 to 1977) seems relevant to recall. Brown recounts her initial impressions of so-called "white feminism" in her book *A Taste of Power*:

"Oddly, I had never thought of myself as a feminist. I had even been denounced by certain radical feminist collectives as a "lackey" for men. That charge was based on my having written and sung two albums of songs that my female accusers claimed elevated and praised men. Resenting that label, I had joined the majority of black women in America in denouncing feminism. **It was an idea reserved for white women,** I said, **assailing the women's movement, wholesale, as either racist or inconsequential to black people.**

Sexism was a secondary problem. Capitalism and racism were primary. **I had maintained that position even in the face of my exasperation with the chauvinism of Black Power men in general and Black Panther men in particular.**" [Emphasis mine]

Directly preceding this excerpt, Brown narrates how a fellow party member had been spreading rumors that she was a "man-hating lesbian" with a "secret sexual life", a charge justified by noting how women had "taken over" the Party. Implicit to these accusations, Brown notes, is not necessarily judgment for *fucking* women.

She had been judged for *valuing* women, for considering them worthy and equal participants in the struggle.

"The feminists were right. The value of my life had been obliterated as much by being female as by being black and poor. **Racism and sexism in America were equal partners in my oppression.**" [Emphasis mine.]

The tale of Brown's eventual exit from the party is an unsavory one. Regina Davis, who according to Brown "held together the proudest of our programs, our school", had been hospitalized with a broken jaw after being beaten by several men in the Party. Brown had called Huey P. Newton to inform him of this, only to be euphemistically notified that he had indeed authorized her "disciplining".

This compelled her to inform Newton of Davis' many tasks and responsibilities, as Brown was sure he didn't realize how indispensable a role Davis played, or was otherwise ignorant of how much she oversaw. She impressed upon Newton that Regina Davis managed everyone from the teachers to the cooks, decided menus and purchases, spoke to parents—"She *is* the fucking school." If Davis had asked a male member of the Party to carry out a task and been refused, Brown stressed that she was well within her rights to verbally reprimand him, and the retaliatory violence Davis had suffered was both disproportionate and alarming.

Newton's response was simply that he already knew everything Brown had told him.

"The Brothers came to me. **I had to give them something.**" [Emphasis mine.]

Televised or not, it seems the revolution will not be gender-inclusive.

From my own perspective as an Indian woman, I can attest that the hollowing out of my land and people is difficult to reckon with, let alone communicate. How do I explain the totalizing impact of mass starvation and centuries of extractivism that continues to this very day, whereby even our modern economy is structured at the behest of neo-imperial interests that treat my people as a nation of sweatshop workers? The widespread poverty plays a huge role in how little agency Indian women are afforded, and every citizen of Empire, irrespective of sex, benefits from the increased standard of living enabled by Third World labor, Third World resources, and goods assembled in the Third World. That is the inescapable impact of racialization, of being deemed worthy for nothing more than serving the White Nation as an external colony of menial workers. Yet, even still ...

Even still.

Even still, it is not the White Woman who is campaigning against the outlawing of marital rape in India.

Yes, white women benefit from the colonial subjugation of brown men and women alike. Yes, I have met more than my fair share of white women who are only too happy to mobilize the violence of racialization to keep me in my place—*trust me*. That does not, in any way, change the reality of brown men—of "our men"—choosing to value continued sexual access to brown women *over our ability to object to it*. It does not alter that in India, economic independence from men continues to be almost impossible for a woman to achieve, even if she does manage to secure more than poverty wages, due to the way single women are locked out of renting or owning property in many places. It does not change that in India, even when we're all brown, women are still *womanized*, still treated as sexual chattel and broodmares and discarded the very moment we cannot fulfill that role.

It does not change that in order to posit dominance feminism as "too essentialist", people will smugly invoke the nature of the relationship between white women and racialized men, while *overlooking racialized women entirely*—just as Crenshaw criticized in *Demarginalizing*, all the way back in the original text of the damn paper in 1989!

That is what intersectionality has been instrumentalized for—*reduced to*, frankly. A theory of expansiveness and inclusion and taking a bottom-up approach to feminist *and* other progressive politics is now most frequently regarded as though it were a theory of fragmentation, as though no woman of color would ever have the temerity and gall to "act white", to demand redress from the patriarchal limitations "her" men subject her to. This is a perversion, a *vandalizing* of intersectionality theory so that marginalized men can deflect and demur when asked to demonstrate *any* contrition or acquiesce to *any* degree of accountability for perpetuating gendered violence against *their* women, *their* rightful sexual chattel to use and abuse as they see fit. A woman of color that asserts herself as a feminist is seen as betraying "her" men, but a man of color that asserts himself as a patriarch betrays nothing and no one—and even succeeds in "reclaiming" some of his "lost masculinity", denied to him by the emasculating forces of white hegemony.

How revolutionary.

Crenshaw concludes her paper with another biting demand for *consistency*—either dominance feminism is no more essentialist for dealing with the plight of the "woman" than antiracist projects are (for homogenizing all racialized subjects without paying mind to intraracial contradictions), or antiracist discourses must also answer for the negligence of the multiply-marginalized subject in their formulation.

There is a right answer here, too. I hope the reader can spot it.

CONCLUSION: RADICAL INTERSECTIONALITY

When I set out to crystallize the thesis of *Brown/Trans/Les*, to decide what I would like my next book on radical transfeminism to be about, I decided to attempt a reconciliation between intersectionality theory and radical feminism. Given the sheer number of people convinced that the twain shall never meet, while nothing about intersectionality precludes or contradicts the precepts of dominance feminism, I thought that it would take at least some work on my part to prove that intersectionality can be easily conceptualized in radical feminist terms. I was wrong.

Because I didn't have to fucking bother.

To anyone familiar with Crenshaw's work, who is aware that she did not stop writing in 1989, who has read her discuss the plight of immigrant women trapped in abusive relationships by male partners who exploit their precarity, this compatibility with radical feminism is no revelation. Crenshaw's work has *always* been feminist, has *always* been informed as much by the indignities of patriarchy as it has by the injustices of racialization. The epistemic vandalism intersectionality has been subject to is the selfsame epistemic vandalism that radical feminism itself has been subject to—that *all* feminism has been subject to, frankly.

If a feminism is found to not adequately serve the interests of patriarchy, it is twisted until it does, or discarded entirely.

On a personal note, I happen to be a trans woman, and thus take great issue with the attempted erasure of womanhood in any avenue. I also, to a certain degree, appreciate that the erasure of multiply-marginalized women from feminist discourses has been widely accepted as epistemic injustice, and that most who would call themselves feminist agree on correcting that error. At the same time, the pervasiveness of this rhetoric in service of discounting or writing feminism off entirely has reduced it to little more than a farce. Activists rebuke feminism on the streets, while in hallowed halls of knowledge-production, the perspectives of multiply-marginalized women are ghettoized into their own fields and topics, or otherwise excluded even still.

Just ask any trans woman who's ever attempted to interface with Women and Gender Studies.

Intersectionality's desecration in this manner is not reflective of a sincere, earnest effort to build an inclusive feminist movement. Rather, the opportunistic leveraging of the very same tendencies the theory critiques is used to destroy solidarity, to say that women who try to come together and identify with each others' struggles are too Essentially

Different to participate in the same, harmonious feminist movement. The Black feminists and the white feminists and the trans feminists and the Third World feminists cannot all relate to the same transcultural, transhistorical struggle against the primacy of male domination in their lives.

So once again, I call *bullshit*.

I'm going to tell you now what drew me to Crenshaw's work, what convinced me of its enduring relevance and indispensability to any and all feminist politics. Underneath all the piercing wit and fearless argumentation and excoriating rhetoric, underneath all the eloquence and articulation, there was buried a primal scream: the primal scream of a woman who navigates a society that knows exactly how to hurt her, surrounded by people who understand everything that harms her perfectly, but still refuse to name or acknowledge the mechanisms by which they do so.

I recognize that scream very, *very* well.

"You *know* what you're doing, and if you won't admit it, then I'll *make* you!"

Multiply-marginalized women have always faced these impulses to align wholly against some subcomponent of the various violences we endure, to be *for* our men, at the behest of race or nation, or to even be for *all* women at the behest of feminists who consider our particular concerns too "divisive". We have always been asked, time and time again, "to whom do you *really* belong?" Who is it that we *really* fight for? To whom do we owe the most loyalty?

To no one who would ask us that question, let me assure you.

I am hers, who reaches across the barriers of time and space and nationhood, who sees my suffering as her own.

I am hers, who walks blasted and blighted pathways that I can and could never, but still sees in me a mirror to her Self.

I am hers, who despite my many errors and missteps, despite my pulling away in anger and fury and despair, reaches through the haze and takes my hand once more, reminding me that we are now inseparable.

I am hers, whose enemies are my enemies and whose battles are my battles, just as hers are mine.

I am hers, who would call me sister, and feel joy when I call her the same.

I am not now, nor will I ever be, anyone's to claim, but I am hers to embrace who would proudly fight at my side.

As she is mine.

3
UNDERSTANDING TRANSMISOGYNY, PART FOUR: PENETRABILITY

How a society so singularly fixated on the phallus manages to be so, so very unsexy.

Before we get started, imagine a straight man, unpleasant though it might be to do so. You likely have a particular image in your head, but consider the following: imagine this man as someone who is exclusively attracted to women, but the only manner of intercourse he engages is the practice colloquially known as "pegging".

Did your mental image of him change at all?

We'll come back to that later.

PHALLOGOMANIA

We have, thus far, variously considered how social dogma becomes layered over empirically observable, tangible subjects. A "woman's biology", her so-called sex, may be "oriented around" gestation, but it does not naturally follow that a human being with the capacity to bear off-spring *must* be feminine, *must* be subordinate and subservient and attracted to those society deems "men", and *must* submit herself to be a mere cog in the regime's natalist machinery. Nor does the *absence* of gestational capacity exempt anyone deemed a 'woman' from misogyny —in fact, this perceived 'defect' marks her, intensifying both scrutiny and repudiation. Many societies third-sex women who cannot be reproductively exploited, irrespective of their actual biological, chromosomal make-up, denying them the title entirely and deeming them worthy for little more than hypersexualization and violence. It is more than evident, then, that *sex* is itself a social designation, a (frequently nonconsensual) *labeling* of an individual to designate their role in societies wholly oriented around male-supremacy. Women are not karyotyped or subjected to X-Rays prior to facing misogyny; their actual anatomy factors far less into their status than advertised.

What, then, truly differentiates patriarchy's two alleged sexes? What is the true *root* of the ideology of sexual difference?

This essay is an admission of an unavoidable truth: that one cannot truly discuss and fully encapsulate sex-the-ideology without reckoning with sex-the-practice. I am, of course, speaking of *fucking*, of *copulating* , of—dare I say it—*intercourse*.

I am not, however, speaking of *all* sexual practices under the sun, and certainly not a great deal of the more stigmatized ones (such as biting). There will be no serious and lengthy meditations on cunnilingus, digital stimulation, mutual masturbation, the incorporation of machinery, or indeed anything actually fun. This is not merely because sex under patriarchy is largely not fun—and not *meant* to be fun—but is also due to the simple fact that only one kind of sex act truly "counts" under a heterosexual regime. There is only one *real* sexual act, and it is this act that both constitutes the social dimension of sex as well as *engenders* it, *sires* it, in a sense.

We are, of course, speaking of *penetration*.

This is a topic we have visited a few times, most explicitly in *Understanding Lesbophobia*, but shall now give all the attention it certainly does not *deserve*, yet receives anyway. Penetration *not* with a finger or tongue or strap-on, and penetration not *of* the mouth or even anus, but good old-fashioned, societally-sanctioned, traditionally-approved god-fearing red-blooded patriotic peepee-goes-in-hooha penetrative sex, the kind that results in *babies*, if all goes well, bless.

Of course, while reproductive utility does factor prominently into this societal sexual calculus, we should be careful to not over-emphasize it. For while doing the babysex to a privately-owned wifemother is the fulfillment of a peepeehaver's natalist, reproductive duty, as well as proof of his vaunted, valorized *virility*, we do live in social contexts that constantly reminds us that the fleshpole and its oft-inconvenient tendency to puff itself up is reflective of a certain runaway, uncontrollable, barely-suppressed libido. (Or at least, that's a good enough excuse to cite when seeking to absolve a member of the Revered Sex-Caste of any sexual violence he may perpetuate.)

One can only support so many families, after all—certainly fewer families than erections—and there is always the troubling conundrum of how one can even maintain one—erection, not family—with all these darned kids running around, leaving our dear wifemother with too little energy and too many headaches. It certainly would be nice if it were possible to enjoy all that sexhaving without having to worry about such boner-killing things as "oops, pregnant again", or "can you seriously not even watch the pot while I change the diapers?!"

As it turns out, the discardable offal with no reproductive utility has a use, after all!

Hierarchical societies that organize their social strata by degrees of dehumanization will always have pools of precarious un-persons from which the most sexually exploitable candidates can be made available to those higher up on the food chain. Whether instrumentalizing poverty, racialization, religiously-mandated inferiority, queerness, or any other stigmatizing and devaluing Mark, societies have always had their *public* women—or close enough—standing in sharp contrast to the respectable, hegemonic, *privatisable* demographics, constituting an underclass of sexual labor that is not deemed *productive*, nor even usually *reproductive*, but some ... third thing.

Here is where one can "maximize their erotic delights", as scholar Adnan Hossein has so nauseatingly put it. While societies have always stigmatized adultery—punishing women more than men, usually—they have also always tolerated it, due to how much sexual access to the gender-marginalized is cherished amongst those men free of gender. Such avenues are rife with permissivity regarding penetration, allowing penetration that is nonprocreative, recreational, and even in some cases, *scandalous*.

What remains constant through all this subversiveness and salacity is that singular maxim: you, who are doing the penetrating, *must not be penetrated*. Well, maybe you can get away with it a little, every now and then, but certainly not where anyone decent might catch wind. If you dare sport the signifiers of masculinity, of gendered *personhood*, of *impenetrability*, you cannot under any circumstance call into question the permanence of your position! Those on top must always be on top, in every sense of the term, because that is what sets them apart, assures their humanity: the ability to breed with seed. Those who aspire to penetrate without the divinely-endowed gift of the meatshaft, and those who turn their backs on that holy gift are both beneath contempt, beneath consideration, and any attempted contravention of this *natural order* that we are enforcing will be *swiftly* dealt with!

Sex-the-ideology thus has an underlying simplicity in much the same way as sex-the-act does, a boiled-down, reductive threshold of acceptability underneath all the modesty, all the moralizing, all the complexities that have sprung up around its enforcement: you're only a person if you possess a penis, and use that penis to penetrate those un-people it's socially acceptable to fuck. We are, therefore, all designated either *penetrators*, who possess the full glory of humanity and agency, or *penetrated*, who are marked for consumption and by that marking rendered subhuman.

In other words: if you were born to be fucked, or like to be fucked, you don't deserve rights.

Let's all just sit with that for a moment.

Because it's every bit as fucking stupid as it sounds.

"SO WHICH ONE OF YOU TAKES IT UP THE ASS?"

A distressing amount of queerphobia sort of snaps into place once you consider penetrability as the lens through which gender is determined. Questions such as "So who's the man and who's the woman?" have always been amusing to gay couples—after the fact, excruciatingly mortifying in the moment—because how absurd it is to ask that about a same-sex relationship! Except, that's not actually what's being asked, insofar as the questioner understands that they're looking at two people who cannot perceptibly be sorted into a heterosexual dyad. What's really being asked is, "So which one of you gets railed, and which one does the railing?"

You know, that common ice-breaker.

This is why heterosexual dynamics appear so quaint to us Enlightened Queers. We do not attach any power or status or verticality to something so mundane as sex acts! We do not consider our value or demeanor or heaven forfend, our *roles* to be defined by how we fuck! We're busy having *sex*, not *gender*! Gender is for the heteros, honey.

I mean ... Well sure, we do have the occasional little in-joke about how tops are like *this*, bottoms are like *that*. And, um, sure, we *do* tend to associate topping with masculinity, with dominance and assertiveness and 'taking the lead' in intimate situations. I suppose the idea of 'top' as the one who penetrates and 'bottom' as the one who receives is in fact widely-accepted lingo, even amongst lesbians who cannot easily class certain sex acts they engage in within this schema (and believe me, during the lesbian sex wars, *they tried*). Also, hm, I do suppose we tend to associate submissiveness, femininity, and a certain desire for objectification ... with ... bottoms ...

Oh, no!

As Judith Butler famously said in *Gender Trouble*, "You can't escape patriarchy, dollface." (I haven't read *Gender Trouble*.) Even amongst queers who play with gender, who consider the taboo and profane to simply be toys to pull out during intercourse, that play-acting is only legible to others insofar as it references or pays homage to or parodies an *existing, established social dynamic*. When we declare our selves, identities, and presentation, when we take to the stage, our gender-performances—no matter how off-script, how improvised, how avant-garde and requiring audience participation—must still be *in a language the audience can comprehend,* because how else are you supposed to have a conversation?

Sadly, when in Rome, we *do* as Romans do.

A quick look at David Valentine's history of gay-lib and trans-lib separation or Esther Newton's *Mother Camp* would disabuse us of more than a few notions of Queer Enlightenment. Gay men's communities were rather unmistakably gendered, with a certain stigma against effeminacy and a certain veneration of the masculine, even as the effeminacy of the penetrable was necessary to define the masculinity of the penetrators by contrast. Even where the subversiveness of gender-play was valued, as amongst drag performers, there was still a certain hierarchy, a disdain expressed for those who "refused to take off the wig", who "took the performance too seriously" and 'crossdressed' full time. The drag queen held the street queen and the hormone queen in low regard, while masculinity remained the prize, worthy of *top* billing even in these putatively non-heterosexual erotic economies.

It would also be quaint to consider gay subcultures—and their associated transsexual subcultures—to be entirely free of gendered anxieties, especially given how the politics of respectability feature in gay civil rights struggles. Notions of 'bottoming leading to effeminacy' prevail both intracommunally and in straight society, with penetrability almost being viewed as a "gateway" to the surrendering of masculinity, of relinquishing one's manhood. These anxieties are reflected just as much in the criminalization of gayness, with some legal regimes historically only penalizing the 'receiver', while continuing to presume the top 'straight', or 'still a man'. Even the term sodomite, as with the terms *faggot, fairy, queen, poof*—they all originated as stigmatizing terms for the penetrable 'male'.

Gayness, then, both within and without, has often been conceptualized as "addicted-to-taking-it-up-the-ass disease", with transsexuality frequently regarded as a particularly *extreme* version of the malady.

Such notions culminated in the 70s and 80s push for gay men to "come out of the closet" *as men*, to affirm that gays could participate in hegemonic masculinity, to leave behind the gender-threat of the screaming queens and streetwalkers. By donning the classy, affluent, manly, manful, fruity-but-only-on-the-weekends-you-know-how-it-is-sugar mask, favor was curried with the heterosexual regime. Gayness was not a disqualifier from citizenship; even gays could uphold and re-inforce reproductive norms; a gay man could be a *man*, not a faggot.

Good for him.

The lesbian version of this took a rather different form, given the way lesbians are typically perceived as women, and so situated some-what differently with respect to masculinity. While (sadly, tragically, re-grettably, heartbreakingly) there was no widespread hierarchization of dyke communities into a butch-archy, the academic lesbian feminist crusade against 'BDSM' and supposedly immoral sexual practices amongst lesbians constructed a rather different stigma.

Indeed, even though they are known principally for trafficking in troonmadness, luminaries no less esteemed than Janice Raymond and Sheila Jeffreys used to babble on about butch-femme relationships as "heterosexual cosplay", about putting a stop to sadomasochistic sex that was 'depoliticizing' lesbian identity and, horror of horrors, turning it into a "lifestyle" that "re-sexualizes" women, making them "worship" the dildo as a "symbol of male power".

You know, it's okay to have a list of limits without trying to out-dyke everyone about it.

There is something truly perverse here, and it's not the strap-ons. While billing themselves as 'radical feminists', Jeffreys, Raymond, and those of their ilk instead chose to reinforce stigmas against female—and especially lesbian—desire, reinventing Catholic guilt for feminists. In their vilification of butches as "male cosplayers"—a prototypical version of the kinds of rhetoric that would be deployed to defame transmasculinity—there is no recognition of how those sexed as women are punished for adopting masculine signifiers, no acknowledgement of the kinds of regendering violence that they are subjected to. Such 'radfems' are the vanguard of a politics characterized by an utter failure of analysis, in favor of pointless moralizing and the unproductive policing of how people like to fuck.

Yet there is some value in their words. After all, sometimes it's good to remember that the people who consider me a fake lesbian discoursed themselves into thinking kinky sex with butches is a sin.

Penetration, then, remains no less a fixture and fixation of queer erotics than it does heterosexual ones. Whether it's gay men desperately holding onto hegemonic manhood by their fingernails or "ex"-Catholics shouting that you're making Lesbian Jesus cry—and in both cases, libeling working-class, gender-bending queer identities to do so —the engendering power of penetration is something we remain subconsciously aware of, even if we struggle to directly name it as a principle determiner of one's *social sex*. The associations formed between dominance, masculine presentation, aggression, agency, and *penetrating*, as well as those formed between submission, effeminacy, passivity, objectification, and *being penetrated*, remain indelible and invisible, but still palpable, almost tangible.

To sum it up in the style of the greatest anonymous philosopher of the digital age: "Taking it up the ass makes you a woman, faggot".

TRANSPENETRABLE

If penetrability was a clarifying lens for parsing some hidden aspects of queer politics and marginalization, it is positively revelatory when applied to transphobia and especially transmisogyny. The recurrent trope of *deception* features heavily in anti-trans propaganda, from the ridiculous notion of 'men dressing up as women' to prey on women in the loos, or the 'trans panic' defense instrumentalized by men to literally get away with murdering us on a plea to temporary insanity, induced by being 'tricked' into sex with transsexual. What engenders this particular anxiety, to the point that trans women become synonymous with *threat*, with *dishonesty*, and so thoroughly excluded from humanity or compassion?

The principle crime trans women stand accused of is adopting the signifiers of the feminine—the *penetrable*—while still being (allegedly) in possession of a *phallus*, that tool of penetration that sets men above all others. The actual presence or absence of one, the actual genital configuration of any given trans woman is immaterial, for the most relevant phallus is the imagined one, the one cis people *believe us to possess* when they think of us and declare us perverts.

It's why the most common question we receive from ignorant and morbidly curious cis people is some version of "Have you had *the surgery?*" *The* Surgery, you know the one, the one that makes you penetrable in the 'proper' way, the one that finally, *actually* makes you a woman, because retaining the ability to penetrate categorically bars you from womanhood no matter how much you are seen, treated, dismissed, decried, and denigrated as a woman in your day-to-day life.

On the other end of the spectrum, these fevered fantasies are also the source of our fetishization, our characterization as *"the best of both worlds"*. A frustratingly common experience for trans women is the reduction of us to *parts*, the carving up of our bodies and beings into an assemblage of sex characteristics for cis people to try and *experiment* with in new and exciting combinations. We are sometimes seen as "starter packs" for queerness, as an *exotic* flavor of gender that might possess some frightening new anatomy that a cis person has heretofore been terrified to interact with, but also bearing some "familiar territory", a gateway to 'ease' oneself through, to *explore* before deciding to *commit*.

In too many cases is the trans woman constructed as a dispenser of "safe" penetration, almost as much as she is considered a "safe", feminized "masculinity" to 'break down' through penetration. Her own feelings about her genitalia—whatever genitalia she may even have—are secondary to the projective fantasies and expectations that are imposed on her, most of which reduce her to "man-lite". She is able to be vilified and deemed sexually improper whether she refuses to penetrate or admits she enjoys it, a perversion of the natural order in either case, whose abjection ensures that no matter whether she fucks or is fucked, she usually does so in a state of disempowerment.

That, then, is the dehumanizing fantasy central to our fetishized sexual appeal: a fantasy of penetration *tamed*, whether we mean coercing it out of an effeminized object and thus defanging its dominant connotations, or diminishing a 'masculine', male personhood by subjecting it to the degradation that is almost inherent to being fucked under patriarchy, where the one fucking you is always primed to extract superiority, agency, and autonomy from the act.

It is also the core of the singular fixation on our sexuality, our *fuckability*, our supposed sexual danger or our hypersexualized vulnerability to exploitation. Cis people, when they think of us, simply cannot stop thinking of our sex—of how we engage in it and who and what we engage in it with, of how we distort and warp their basic assumptions about our collective sexed reality—and then blame *us* for *their* extreme reactions of disgust or desire (or frequently, *both*). To paraphrase Dworkin, trans women *are* sex, are inseparable from sex, because we are reduced to nothing but our capacity for risky, exotic, transgressive, boundary-breaking, taboo, forbidden, unholy sex, by cis people who call us sickos because *they* can't stop thinking about our dicks.

Cool.

SEXUAL LIB-ERATION

You know, it's almost funny how important *shame* is.

Grand theories of oppression and structural forces, while useful in conceptualizing the machinery of mundane evils, sometimes render the picture a bit too *clean*, a bit too *clinical*. Yes, there are incentives, just as there is power, labor, and unequal material conditions that enable some to secure these more easily than others. There is also, however, messiness and contradiction and ambiguity, a dozen-and-a-half failure states and fudged boundaries and imperfections that absolute decrees of dichotomous sex and heterosexual primacy paper over unrigorously. Sometimes, anything that makes a man's dick hard is a woman. Sometimes, that same erection is a source of uncertainty, of destabilization, of questions that a rigidly-delineated patriarchal ideology does not have satisfying or reassuring answers to.

Shame is the shallow pool where trannies are drowned.

Those trans panic defenses are used by lovers and boyfriends, you know. By men who know perfectly well that the woman they're sleeping with is trans, who have slept with her before, even, or specifically sought out a trans woman to bed, but whose internal discord about their own identity and sexuality becomes violently externalized (as is common for men), or who fear their amorous activities being discovered by friends or family and so elect to capitalize on transfeminine disposability instead of sending a fucking break-up text. I think of these men in the same vein as I think of those men who kill their families and then themselves—usually when a battered wifemother tries to leave—and I wonder, yet again, why the violence they commit must spill beyond the only deserving target.

To be penetrable is to be a receptacle for the sins of the impenetrable, a vessel for their grief and turmoil and especially, especially their despair and rage.

There's plenty of shame to go around for the penetrable too, more than enough. The shame of being a feminist and guiltily enjoying being *demeaned* and *tainted* and *ruined*, of feeling like you're letting down the sisterhood with every paroxysmal thrust. The shame of batting a hand away only to have '*tease*' spat at you, wondering whether you were, in fact, a little too flirty, a little too provocative, whether you did in fact send mixed signals—didn't you, really, ask for it? The shame of expressing desire only to be told you're disgusting for it, the shame of failing to be the proper, modest woman you're supposed to be, or the shame of being too prudish and frigid and puritanical instead of the proper, sexually-liberated woman you're supposed to be, or just the fucking bone-deep never-ending inexhaustible shame of being born not in the wrong *body*, but the wrong fucking *society*, a society where there's just no right way for you to *be*.

That pool might be a bit deeper than initially advertised.

I worry sometimes that over the past few decades, feminism at some point stopped being about agitation and action and advocacy and analysis, and became a politics of how best to live with ourselves. Of how to manage the shame that comes with being—what, a woman, an object, a victim, a temptress, an inspiration, a girlboss, a goddess, a mother, a pedestalized muse—being a lot of things, but never *enough*. I have witnessed the development of feminist politics without much explanatory value, but with a lot of comfort, a lot of telling each other, "We're doing fine, we're not doing anything wrong, we're not evil for having desires. It's not a betrayal of anyone or anything if I'm an unrepentant slut or a devout of the faith or an aspiring housewife. It's *my choice*."

There's more value in that than some of us are willing to admit.

Liberal-feminist dreams of empowerment through intercourse did not catch on because they were without merit or appeal. Our desires, our libidos, our primal urges that are a reflexive, unconscious expression of what we refuse to admit we *truly* want, are aspects of ourselves that we have been taught to be constantly at war with. It is so, so very tempting, then, to reach out and join hands and ask for a collective reckoning with the stigma and *shame* of sex, to ask that this most intimate practice, most intimate expression of love and companionship and fealty and togetherness be rendered finally free of society's judgment.

The idea is really, really compelling.

Unfortunately.

Unfortunately, the stakes are not the same for everyone.

While 'shame' is indeed relevant—one might even say *central*—to sexual politics, it is also obfuscating. For the shame that the penetrable struggle with is the shame tied to navigating a series of contradictory directives that determine the sum total of our worth. Are we *loose*, too-freely available for use by any and every Thomas, Henry, or especially Richard? Or are we too unavailable, too difficult to make *submit*, and thus too jealously guarding an ultimately common resource—*fuckability*—that can easily be acquired elsewhere, so not *worth* the trouble? These questions hang over us because even in societies that purport to have moved past the equivocation of our humanity to our sexual availability, and to our management of the "correct" level of access to our bodies, peeking 'under the hood' reveals that pretense to be little more than theater.

Meanwhile, the penetrators are less concerned with destigmatizing sex and more with securing their position as sexual consumers. *Their* shame stems from wishing to ward off any possible similarity or association with those they are meant to use. Become too much like us, lose too much of that fleshpole-swinging swagger that assures one's place in the hierarchy of "who inserts the dongle", and suddenly they face that unenviable fate that they have relegated the rest of us to. The shame that gets trannies killed is about patriarchal mores and deep-set insecurities and the struggle to reconcile proscribed desires with self-image, but it's also a shame that manifests as violence specifically because any 'temptation', any 'deviation' from the strictures of impenetrability are to be purged from those who wish to continue navigating the world as dominant, as autonomous—as *people.*

No matter how much we try to reclaim the word 'slut', we ultimately still wrestle with social norms where the burdens of sexual access—and condemnation for it—reside entirely with those deemed penetrable, whose very presence is invitation, whose very existence is a risk of violation.

You can't escape patriarchy, dollface.

CONCLUSION: YES, I WEAR PANTS

Penetrability, then, is distinct from *heterosexuality* (despite being derived from it) because it is the connective tissue linking a series of associations we all bear in mind when navigating the sociality of sex. *Masculine presentation* is correlated with *male 'identification', 'male' anatomy, dominance* in both personality and intimacy, and a presumption of *impenetrability* during intercourse. The disruption of these correlations gives rise to a series of dynamics and anxieties that typify an expansive notion of "queerness", insofar as it is understood to be a subversion, disruption, or contravention of patriarchal sexual norms.

Penetrability is what makes the idea of 'pegging', of a masculine, manly, manful man 'taking it', into a 'slippery slope' to effeminization and faggotry and oh my stars, maybe even transsexual woman-identification. The importance of securing one's impenetrability, as well as the ease with which it can be stripped away, is what makes our heterosexual male bottom from the beginning of this essay such a macabre curiosity. While such an individual *can*—and likely even *does*—exist, he is what an insufferable scholar might call "queered" by his, ahem, 'inversion' of the sexual role he is meant to embody, even if he looks like Henry Cavill and gets railed by supermodels.

To allow yourself 'to be used', *like a woman,* is to risk surrendering all that makes you part of the dominant sex-caste.

Conversely, penetrability is why sexual absurdities are replicated in queer communities that are ostensibly free of them, making something as simple as a non-stone butch invite ridicule from queer theorists like Jack Halberstam. In *Female Masculinity*, Halberstam firmly equivocates butch identity with 'stone butch' identity—that is, a masculine (implicitly cissexual, non-transfem) lesbian who is a touch-me-not and only engages in intercourse by penetrating their partner. In this context, a penetrable butch appears as a *question:*

"... the question is not really why would a butch not want to be touched but rather how do butches switch between being masculine on the streets and female in the sheets?"

Here, 'masculine' means *to present masculine*, while 'female in the sheets' is a too-clever-by-half euphemism for being penetrated. I frankly think such an existence is not contradictory in the slightest, but anxieties around penetrability do not inform my entire sense of self.

Not that transfem identity or existence is "beyond" the binary of penetrability—far from it. Though our sexual objectification as subversive oddities is rooted in being penetrable when we're not "supposed" to be, or in penetrating with the signifiers of those who "shouldn't", the transmedicalist gatekeeping of our transition care is very rigorously oriented around producing the perfect, penetrable subject. Historically, we must be hyperfeminine, hyperhetero, and hyper-gung-ho about our desire to be traditional homemakers and decorative ornaments for masculine, manful, manly, impenetrable men, if we are to stand any chance of medical institutions permitting our transitions.

It's why the wider world knows me first as "cross-dressing pervert", not "lesbian".

This is the point in the essay where I dazzle and titillate my readers in equal measure through a salacious confession of just how many *boundaries* I *transgress* and how many *norms* I *queer* through sheer proximity, but if you'll pardon the expression: I just don't give a fuck. The status of my genitals, relationships, methods of intercourse or the people I engage in it with can be as varied and exotic or banal and vanilla as you please. What practices of intimacy I *actually* engage in do not matter one whit to a wider culture that has never cared about individual queers, and I remain, no matter what I do, a curiosity, an exhibit, a freakshow for cissexist, heterosexual perspectives to project all their fantasies and fears onto.

No perfectly executed move by me is going to snap the patriarchy in half, no matter how much I will it so.

No, the scourge of penetrability is historical, long-reaching, and firmly embedded into the innermost recesses of our psyches and puns. There is no surgery I can get for decoupling penetration from aggression and agency and domination, or for washing away the devaluation of the penetrated. That part of trans existence—of being women, of *being* sex, *of being gender*—we just have to live with.

Unless.

Unless, unless, unless.

Good intentions only go so far. Sticks and stones may break our bones, but whips and chains have their limitations, too. Combating shame is crucial, relevant, important—but it's not paramount.

You also have to do the work.

To organize. To recognize who is invested in your subjugation and who isn't. To capitalize on opportunities to build solidarities, coalitions, and movements, without centering everything on individual *choice* or individual *trauma*. To confront—legally, socially, and politically—those who seek to exploit and extract from you, and to build a world where this entire meditation on penetrability becomes an anachronism.

I really, really hope we get there. If not in this lifetime, then the next.

Because I just want to enjoy being a dyke, y'all. The rest of this shit is *such* a buzzkill.

4
UNDERSTANDING TRANSMISOGYNY, PART FIVE: NATALISM, NATIVISM, NATIONALISM

Content Warning: *Discussions of genocide, eliminationism, sexual violence, and the bloodshed inherent to nation-building. When discussing vulgar ideologies, we must sometimes frankly discuss their vulgar ideas in plain language.*

> *"The conversion of Muslim woman to Hinduism and of Hindu woman to Islam looked at from a social and political point of view cannot but be fraught with tremendous consequences. It means a disturbance in the numerical balance between the two communities. As the disturbance was being brought about by the abduction of women, it could not be overlooked.* **For woman is at once the seed-bed of and the hothouse for**

nationalism in a degree that man can never be.
These conversions of women and their subsequent
marriages were there-fore regarded, and rightly, as a
series of depredations practised by Hindus against
Muslims and by Muslims against Hindus **with a view to**
bringing about a change in their relative numerical
strength. *"* [Emphasis mine.]

– Dr. B. R. Ambedkar, *Partition of India*

BREEDER LOGIC

'The Great Replacement' is a conspiracy theory popular amongst white supremacists and neo-Nazis in the West. It is an interesting case study in exactly what kinds of logic are needed to prop up myths of innate, inherent superiority while justifying persecution and violence against marginalized groups as an act of self-defense. Most versions of the conspiracy talk about some manner of shadowy, secretive group with outsize power—"elites", "the deep state", "cabals" and the like— orchestrating the "decline of the white race" through the manipulation of demographic shifts.

Think of the "stabbed in the back" myth in post-World War One Germany. The great, powerful, imperially superior Nation was not defeated on the battlefield, because its military might was without question and its power without equal. Rather, the Nation was defeated because it was *betrayed, deceived, undermined, sabotaged* by seditious internal elements, who used "underhanded" and "dishonorable" tactics to orchestrate a defeat "from within". Jews and socialists are the classical scapegoats targeted by such anti-National accusations, but the utility of this myth is in its flexibility: it can be directed at whichever group it is most convenient to presently slander.

Today, 'The Great Replacement' largely accuses our supposed shadowy overlords of enacting various schemes towards 'population control', specifically to curb the numbers of white people. The most visible and mainstream manifestation of these politics is the immigrant panic sweeping the West. A 2022 article in The Guardian discusses how this idea, once a fringe far-right conspiracy, has increasingly become a fixture of mainstream right-wing politics in the West, echoed and alluded by figures such as Fox News' Tucker Carlson and Hungary's Prime Minister, Viktor Orbán. It is, at its heart, a *demographic anxiety*: a concern that other people, other cultures will become more numerous, more populous, more relevant, more *normative* than you and yours.

It is the fear of becoming a minority.

This turn against immigration illustrates a contradiction at the heart of Western neoliberal policies that has enabled the popularisation of fascist rhetoric. Immigrants serve as a source of precarious, cheap labor in Western nations, whether we mean Mexican farmworkers, Filipino nurses, or even Indian tech workers. Their tenuous legal status can be exploited to prevent them from organizing effectively for higher wages, as the simple prospect of earning an income in dollars (or euros or pounds) is attractive when compared to meager economic prospects in their neocolonised countries of origin.

Immigrant labor, then, allows capitalists to undercut homegrown labor pools and even provides them with a ready scapegoat for stagnant wages. Rather than viewing immigrants as fellow workers being (super-)exploited by the same regimes, nativist political sentiment is quick to divide along racial and national lines. The very source of cheap labor becomes a political wedge issue, and economies in a death spiral (such as the post-Brexit UK) demand the expulsion of workers upon whom the entire national infrastructure now depends. Fascism is always effective in disrupting worker solidarity, certainly, but it rarely turns out good for business overall.

Then again, I'm making the mistake of assuming wealthy capitalists, especially the modern techno-libertarian sort, have any interest in preserving a functional society.

Replacement conspiracies are, ultimately, rooted in the most primal fears about the external Other. Most societies have internal hierarchies to enforce and external threats to keep at bay, whether real or imagined. Replacement conspiracies stoke fears of a fragile order coming undone, of an unholy alliance between saboteurs and malcontents within and savages and barbarians without, joining forces to make the People of the Great Nation—the *volk*, if you will—an underclass in their 'own home'. It is the recurring nightmare of a society founded in and perpetuated by blood meeting its end the same way.

Many far-right fixations stem from and converge upon this singular fear. We must fearmonger about the encroaching savage hordes, certainly, but what about the pollution and rot tainting our own people's "genetic purity", or the Nation's "racial hygiene"? Feminism, queer rights, critical race theory, 'DEI'—it is all trivially spun into the newest iteration of 'cultural Marxism' or 'Judeo-Bolshevism' or whatever the reactionary euphemism du jour is. After all, if the volk are going to be *outbred* by inferior people, we need to do everything we can to *ensure the continuation of our race*, and *a future for our children*, shall we say (in fourteen words or less).

Think of how far feminism has gone, for instance. Women can be or do anything these days, except the one thing they're *meant* to be, the one thing they're *supposed* to do: motherhood! Bearing and birthing and raising the Nation's very future, fulfilling their reproductive duty to their lineage and doing their part in ensuring the next generation preserves The Nation's values. They need to be mothers to the *right* sort of children and wed the *right* sort of men, of course. The more-liberal eras tried this entire 'multiculturalism' business, but the politics of the day call for insularity, knowing that any attempt by different peoples to live in harmony is doomed to failure.

It must thus be observed how dangerous it is to allow women to do things like become literate, own property, and choose their own partners without familial intervention. Look how lonely the men are now! Look at how precipitously the birthrates are falling, how many immigrants are proliferating, how women are even sleeping with and marrying *each other*, wasting two perfectly good wombs at once! This simply cannot be allowed to go on.

The Conservative Political Action Committee, or CPAC, is a right-wing US group that held a special meeting in Budapest in 2022, to promote ties between the GOP and the aforementioned Viktor Orbán. At this special meeting, CPAC's chairman Matt Schlapp had this to say:

"If you say there is a population problem in a country, but you're killing millions of your own people through legalized abortion every year, if that were to be reduced, some of that problem is solved ... If you're worried about this quote-unquote replacement, why don't we start there? Start with allowing *our own people* to live." [Emphasis mine.]

These statements were made mere months before *Roe v. Wade* was overturned by the US Supreme Court.

Replacement theories, then, illustrate a crucial facet of fascist politics: the necessity to frame the persecution of the marginalized as a defense of the Nation, especially in times of peace, when there is no war to propagandise, to mobilise and unite the volk. Justifying reactionary violence is a psychological necessity, for even those who delight in cruelty and exploitation still often feel the need to see themselves as in the right, to frame their own actions as righteous, as an unsavory necessity that might not be "pretty", but "must be done" for the sake of the "greater good". Powerless groups are recast as deceptive elites, or dehumanized instruments of a greater, secret will, whose inferiority and rapaciousness is not their fault, as such, but an innate part of their nature that demands their culling. Replacement myths are how asylum-seekers and refugees fleeing war-torn lands become an invading force on Western shores, how displaced and destroyed communities become cartels and criminals and terrorists.

It's how the powerful silence their own conscience while killing the helpless.

MAIDEN, MOTHER, DRONE

The 'Cross of Honor of the German Mother' was an award issued by the government of Nazi Germany to 'worthy mothers'—that is, those women who had fulfilled their duty to the Nation by birthing more than four children. The medals came in bronze, silver, and finally gold, for those select mothers who had borne and raised over eight children in accordance with Nazi values. To be eligible, the mother and father of the children had to both be of "pure German blood", of course, and "genetically healthy". The point of the award was to incentivize and propagandize the image of the woman as the womb of the Nation, the cradle of the Volk's future, whose fecundity is her greatest asset and her greatest contribution to the National project.

This is the place that reactionary politics carves out for women (the *cis* is implicit, and the *heterosexual* is mandated). A place of dubious honor as "the seed-bed of nationalism", as Ambedkar put it. It is a meager reward, consisting of menial work, reduced autonomy, financial dependence and monotonous drudgery, but it is at least better than the alternative. Especially in climates where women's financial prospects are limited and their independence restricted, subsuming one's existence into "someone's wife and mother" is as good as the deal gets.

Such a poisoned pill forms the basis of many a reactionary feminism. Women of the non-hegemonic demographic, queer women, disabled women, and so on have their interests sidelined and diminished in favor of the politics of female status, by women who can secure their place as favored broodmares in a Nationalist order. Those who cannot must simply be discarded, relegated to a lower tier as a sexually exploitable underclass, deemed reproductively worthless due to their capacity to gestate the Nation's ideal citizens, and so consigned to absorbing the sexual violence that men simply must indulge in.

It then becomes obvious that *reproduction*—and control over it—forms a central fixation of reactionary, conservative, and Nationalist politics. Even in the case of the most privileged, hegemonic groups, the size of the population remains a concern, something for the state to manage and weigh against the size of every other population within the Nation's internal hierarchy. This is why the neo-Malthusian politics that were a recent fad, raising concerns about global overpopulation and resource depletion as a response to the looming ecological crises, have seamlessly given way to elite scaremongering about the "replacement rate", about Western nations not reproducing enough, about lonely men and educated women and no-fault divorce and abortion being too-freely available. Woman is the "hothouse for nationalism", which is why she must be so strictly controlled, managed, constrained, directed—treated as a natural resource, almost, a vital asset that the Nation cannot afford to squander.

Why do Western nations so concerned about replacement rates and having enough workers to do the essential labor of maintaining society still participate in immigrant panics, despite immigration being a ready, efficient solution to the problem? Despite population redistribution remedying both "overpopulation" and "underpopulation" simultaneously? Because the immigrants are not the *right* kind of citizen, not the *right* kind of laborer—reproductive or otherwise! Regimes dependent on hierarchies wish to perpetuate said hierarchies, wish to rely on the loyalty of those who have always been elevated at the expense of others, and cannot make do with the proliferation of the lesser, the inferior, those of 'tainted blood' who definitionally cannot bear or birth the full-blooded genetically pure proud Men of the Nation! (Proud Boys, even.)

This obsession with ensuring the proliferation of *productive* citizens of the regime, defined as 'loyal' and sufficiently 'able' members of the hegemonic demographic, easily gives rise to eugenical politics and policies. Disability and sickness almost becomes treason, then, an inexcusable diminishment in one's capacity to Serve The Nation. All deviation from the ideal in turn becomes *deviancy*, insufficiency and lack becoming a moral failure, a malicious non-compliance with ruling-class aims to preserve the 'natural order' that props up their power. Is being queer in a heterosexual Nation a crime? Is being non-white in a White Nation a defect? It might as well be, says the Supremacist, the Patriarch, the *Patriot*—and it certainly is treated so.

Womanhood, then, is defined patriarchally as *wombynhood*, as the duty every True Citizen with a uterus is expected to uphold. You must birth our Nation's leaders—and also its soldiers, its enforcers, its cops, its middle-managers, its zealots and supremacists and priests and future wombs, too. You must raise them to be as invested in the Nation as you yourself no doubt are, and for your service, your dedication of mind, body, and ideology to your regime, we will award you a *MutterKreuz*, or a *Médaille de l'enfance et des familles*, or an *Orden Materinskaya Slava*. You will be recognized as someone who bore her charge of servitude well.

Mean though this recognition is, throughout history we have found women who will nonetheless clamor for it, tear each other apart for it, and forge their entire sense of self around being a *respectable, venerated* Mother and not, you know, some cheap floozy dime-a-dozen *harlot*. This is the foundation of modesty politics, the patriarchal buy-in to 'proper womanhood' enforced by men and women alike: Be a womb, or be a hole.

After all, if you're going to be treated as less than a full human regardless, would you rather not be treated like an un-person with *some* dignity? Some *use*?

Or would you rather be treated like *them*?

DERELICTION OF DUTY

There are many ways to fail the State.

If Nationalism is understood as a politics of constructing and upholding hierarchies, as the promotion of in-groups to preserve and outgroups to punish or exploit, then the function of patriarchy becomes plain as day, as a vital social technology deployed to secure, retain and police *essential* reproductive assets. It explains the 'martial disposability' of men, in terms of who can be allowed to wage war without overly threatening the Nation's demographic future, as well as the targeting of women during genocide in sexually violent ways that frequently involve mutilation of their sexual characteristics.

To refuse to gestate is a betrayal of the Nation—hence the conservative attempts to regulate abortion, contraception, and women's freedom to exist autonomously. To bear a child for the out-group is perhaps an even greater betrayal, as it is not only a denial of your reproductive potential to your country, but a commitment to furthering the cause of the Other.

Queer existence too falls somewhere in that neighborhood. Imagine the temerity of women who think they can claim each other as a man claims a woman, locking both into a non-reproductive coupling! Gay men are beaten and reviled and made examples of, while lesbians are denied existence, epistemically erased to a degree that their very possibility is disallowed. For an unclaimed woman is always just an unclaimed woman, waiting for her utility to the Nation to be suitably exploited, until the age where her value expires and she is relegated to the gendered trash-heap with all the others.

Queerness, then, is treated as *desertion*, as a dereliction of duty, an act of treason that can practically render a person stateless, loyal to no regime, a burden and layabout refusing to do their reproductive duty. If reproductive roles are what give humans value, purpose, and designations in terms of how they must labor, then queerness is a refusal, a non-compliance with patriarchal strictures positing that we are more than the base, mammalian instinct to multiply—that human value is not the sole purview of the sire, the impregnator, the *Man*, and is in fact detached entirely from how and whether we reproduce.

It is a degree of temerity and insubordination that no patriarchy, no Nation can deign to tolerate.

Discussions of 'gay assimilation' often use terms like "respectability", or "middle-class values", or some abstract encapsulation of the idea that the split between liberation and assimilation occurs along classed or racial lines. While affluence and proximity to hegemonic demographics no doubt play a crucial role, it is more illuminating to think about the fight for gay rights—specifically gay recognition, gay marriage—in terms of *compliance*. A gay man in a crisp suit and a lesbian in a suitably flowery dress, irrespective of their specific status or identity, distinguish themselves from their rowdier, sluttier, more *deviant* and *deviating* counterparts through gender-conformity, through the promise (and the lie) that sexuality and gender are perfectly discrete and separable constructions. "Even if we are men coupled with men, or women coupled with women," goes the refrain, "we are *still men and women.*"

Reproduction lies at the heart of gay assimilation, or gay liberalism, or gay citizenship, if you will. A willingness to reproduce the Nation's ideals, and a willingness to reproduce *as men and women*. Lesbians with sperm donors, gay men with surrogates, or both with adoption— all technologies of reproductive justice that conservatives oppose due to their fetish for the 'natural'—enable gay citizens to avoid becoming truly *queer*. And so, the patriarchy finds a bargain for yet another gender-marginalized group—tenuous and limited to specific socio-economic climes though it may be.

Therein lies the source of the split between an attempt to fashion a "GLB" politics that "drops the T"—though, make no mistake, a trans politics of affluence most definitely exists. It resides in the negotiations trans people have tried to make with medical professionals, to be perfect gender-conforming stereotypes of our "chosen gender" in exchange for the permission and means to bodily transition. Even still, even if trans people participate in reproduction both ideological and sexual, it remains the case that transition itself is an unforgivable patriarchal sin, a demonstration of porosity between sexed categories that can never be given official sanction. Gay citizens bow and scrape for their pittance of gender-deviation, to be allowed to love whoever they wish, but promise to uphold that Man and Woman have meaning, remain distinct categories that can never be superseded and ignored. Trans people, even if we swear to behave once we've "crossed", still need to make the crossing, and so reveal that such a crossing is possible.

An impudence that has no place in a civilized, patriarchal society.

The reproductive anxieties inherent to transphobia—both in the sense of illustrating the farce of patriarchal male-supremacy, and in the scaremongering notion of bodily transition as a form of 'mutilation' that destroys a perfectly healthy citizen's reproductive viability—are very apparent in those who peddle the trans panic. A remarkably recent article (as of time of writing) on http://redstate.com/, entitled *The Transgender Breeding Program Is One of the Most Sinister Plots in History*, spells out the derangement trans people inspire in the conservative id quite thoroughly.

While it was no doubt written with one hand—the article mentions "corruption kink", for crying out loud—it blessedly does not devolve into lurid speculation about trans people's dating habits. Rather, it consolidates a specific image of the 'threat' trans people pose to polite, heterosexual society, constructed via breathless repetition in the works of obsessives such as Janice Raymond, Abigail Shrier, and the UK Gender-Conservative movement. Trans people cannot reproduce, the false claim goes, and so trans people are interested in *recruiting and stealing your child*! It is a remix of the groomer panic that was once directed at gay people, relegating trans existence to the purely libidinal for the sake of portraying us as rapacious, heterosexuality-destroying monsters.

Amidst all this vilification, there is an interesting admission in the article, though.

"Ideologies thrive in different ways, but the best is environmental conditioning. *This happens all the time in family settings*, where the child is born and raised in a home where the ideology typically becomes the standard. *This can be undermined, however,* and often is by *outside forces* and nearly always when the subject is young and impressionable." [Emphasis mine.]

Such a casual admission—that conservative, patriarchal, heterosexual indoctrination is an ideology that must be instilled in children, and *can be undermined*—occurs because it doesn't even register as one. This is simply what conservatives regard as normal, even if they dedicate so much more propaganda and violence into spreading and maintaining their vision of the world than queer people ever could, or would even want to. They understand that patriarchy is not *natural* or *hard-wired*, but consider its defense so vital to their identity and indeed *ideology*, that the escalating persecution of a vilified minority and resorting to the abuse of one's own children are perfectly acceptable conditions to that end.

That is why an absolute majority of messaging targeting the parents of trans kids is conservative fearmongering, misinformation, and advice on how to restrict children's autonomy, or otherwise harm them if they persist in identifying as trans. The United Kingdom's Secretary of State for Health, Wes Streeting, has met with pro-conversion therapy groups like Bayswater, whose members include parents willing to put "extra hot chili sauce" in their trans child's eye makeup. He has not, however, met with any trans groups or trans youth, even as he persists in upholding the UK's puberty blockers ban for trans children (and trans children only), a ruling based in dubious and shoddy research.

A final interesting feature of the Red State article is the framing of who is engaging in these child-stealing activities. The author reiterates the conservative fixation on the normalization of drag and events such as 'Drag Queen Story Hour', which are innocuous gatherings where an adult reads a story out to children. The only thing that makes it "obscene" in the eyes of a conservative is the adult in question being a man in drag, a man who presents differently than he ought to, which is the category that all trans women are routinely collapsed into by bad-faith actors.

This, paired with Abigail Shrier's narrative of *Irreversible Damage*, of a "transgender fad" targeting "young teenage girls" into "mutilating themselves" and supposedly destroying their future gestational capacity or ability to orgasm (both bunk), paints a very particular picture of adult, "sexually deviant men" targeting and allegedly victimizing these supposed young girls, casting trans women specifically as a kind of rapacious male threat to the Nation's precious reproductive assets. In that regard it is homoousian with many a xenophobic or racialized panic, borrowing from and building on tropes that position the Nation's women as a prize, a form of wealth that men of the out-group covet and seek to despoil, pollute, or steal away.

That is how the reactionary, fascistic, Nationalist conceptions of gender, race, and queerness *intersect*. They are overlapping and mutually reinforcing social technologies whose purpose is to construct a hierarchy of citizenship, of loyalty, of fealty to the Nation and its ideological obsession with reproduction. Through this lens, we can see how the struggles of women, queer people, and colonised people are all inherently the same struggle, interconnected and mutually reinforcing, proving that we all benefit from coming together and advocating for our shared interests against the hegemony oppressing us all. These groups are, therefore, natural allies in the worldwide struggle against imperialism, colonialism, and patriarchy.

... Right?

INTERLUDE: "TRANSMISOGYNY IS WHITE SUPREMACY"

A 2024 report by the Global Network on Extremism and Technology, entitled *Transmisogyny, Colonialism and Online Anti-Trans Activism* has an interesting section, *A Postcolonial Approach to Anti-Trans Activism*, where it states:

"Analysing online anti-trans activism through the framework of coloniality, we argue, makes clear that transphobia generally, and transmisogyny specifically, are *foundational to European and North American ideas of how society should be organised* and who is allowed to commit violence. Considering coloniality allows us to *demonstrate the innate white supremacy of transphobia: rooted in settler colonialism, tightly prescribed gender roles made colonised societies simpler to understand and easier to control.* Trans people, and particularly trans women, not only challenge these gender roles, but they expose them as roles chosen by colonisers rather than natural states of being." [Emphasis mine.]

This certainly seems to naturally follow from what we've discussed so far. If a white-supremacist society's conception of gender involves rigid ideas of reproduction, to the point of making it obligate, then naturally non-white societies can never perform "gender" to an imperialist standard's satisfaction, because they produce no white babies.

Some scholars would go so far as to argue that racialization innately "queers" people, given that whiteness enforces global standards.

It's a fascinating line of inquiry, one that compels me to ask a question that I promise is not a trick question, but one that simply must be asked given the premises we're working with. If racialization queers non-white people... does that mean that white trans people are racialized?

That is, do white trans people... experience racism?

Have a think. We'll come back to that one.

GENDER ISN'T (JUST) WHITE

A few months ago, my co-host and I had the pleasure of sitting down to record an episode of our podcast, *Cracked Ivory*, with Jude Doyle. We were interviewing Jude about his book, *Did I Leave Feminism?*, a semi-autobiographical treatise on his relationship to feminism as a trans man, and re-evaluation of the orthodoxies that have dominated trans politics and advocacy. It is a sharp, lucid and welcome intervention, and we talked at length about why Jude, like many other transfeminists, is giving the second wave a second look these days.

However, there was one aspect of Jude's text that I came across, that I felt the need to question him more on. Consider the following snippet from the very first chapter, *Gender*:

"Still, globally, or in terms of the contemporary consciousness, patriarchy and its binary gender scheme dominate the narrative. It's so pervasive that many of us, including many feminists, assume it's the way things have always been. How did this happen? The short answer is 'white people.' The longer answer, which still amounts to 'white people,' is colonialism and the Catholic church.

We still don't know why European Christian culture became so heavily invested in patriarchy—it is partially, though probably not only, a matter of cultural inheritance from ancient Greece and Rome—but the historical record shows us that where white colonizers go, patriarchy follows. This does not happen solely through nebulous cultural influence, or even through propaganda spread by Christian missionaries (though both play a role) but through actual laws passed to prohibit egalitarian societal arrangements. In places where inheritance passed down through the female line, colonized subjects would be required by law to start willing their property to their sons. In places where women traditionally ruled, the colonizers would force them to hand their titles down to male heirs.

Whole civilizations had their histories rewritten to make patriarchy appear universal and inevitable." [Emphasis mine.]

This idea of patriarchy as a colonizing force is related to my own work on trying to elucidate the transnational contours of racialized transmisogyny, and is a perspective that I have repeatedly encountered amongst Western trans activists and scholars. Jude is not and should not be treated as a representative spokesman for Western trans activism, but as he was someone who had just finished writing a book about Western transfeminism, I chose to ask him the following question:

"One thing that's of personal relevance to my work is the degree of epistemic extractivism the Western academy subjects non-Western queer populations too, re-imagining non-Western societies as gender-expansive or post-patriarchal in ways that do not really map to reality. The main example I've discussed in the past is the rather orientalist view of India's hijra that is mainstream in the West. Some of this has been facilitated by diaspora and non-Western scholars who pin the blame for non-Western patriarchy entirely on colonization or otherwise make empirically dubious claims about their societies' relationship to gender and queerness. I wanted to ask you about what it would mean for Western trans scholarship to reckon with the reality of non-Western patriarchy and have to retreat from these claims of "binary gender" being a purely Eurocolonial purview."

Jude gave an answer that I very much appreciated, and I hope I can convey that even when challenged, he approaches topics with a lot of thoughtfulness and insight. What remains true, however, is that many writers and scholars in trans studies, queer theory, and wider decolonial studies—note that I did not say 'white', deliberately—remain married to a conception of gender as a "white invention", as a tool of settler-colonialism that was *externally imposed* on the catch-all of "non-Western cultures".

It begs the question: Was white, Christian colonialism the reason that in 10th Century China, young girls had their feet broken and tightly, painfully bound to make them appear smaller and more dainty? Were time-travelling Christian patriarchs the reason that the *Laws of Manu*, a Hindu text, talks about how wives are to always defer to husbands, and how 'eunuchs' are unclean?

More importantly: Why are the supposed foremost scholars on the cutting edge of gender, queerness and feminism so beholden to making such reductive, absurd, and easily disprovable claims about patriarchy?

It's a claim that's repeated casually in online queer spaces, by Western queers who have an incredibly quaint idea of what life in the Third World is like. It's also repeated in Emma Heaney's *Feminism Against Cisness*, a collection whose first essay by Cameron Awkward-Rich talks about the co-optation of Sojourner Truth by white trans activists, and whose *second* essay by Kristjansson and Heaney espouses this reductive view of all non-Western societies, whose disparate histories are being homogenized and co-opted for the benefit of Western trans studies!

Much like the orientalism and moral relativism surrounding the "third-gender" idea applied to racialized trans women across the third world, this mythologized non-patriarchal wonderland that exists outside the boundaries of white, Christian, imperial society and instantly collapses on contact with it is just a rhetorical tool, an instrumentalization of complex histories and struggles—of caste, creed, queerness, and *yes*, gender!—into a fairy tale for Enlightened Queers to repeat at bedtime. It is a refusal to reckon with the patriarchal realities of nations that were innovating ways to impoverish and marginalize transsexuals aeons before 'Europe' was even a coherent concept. It is, bluntly, not merely historically and morally irresponsible, but also a giant cop-out by people who are whole-heartedly reinforcing the notion of the non-West as a preserved, primitive "living past" from which modern white, Western, Christian society can glean a lot of valuable lessons on how best to live!

Simply put, it's an utter erasure of the oppression of women of color across the globe for the purpose of telling a more flattering story.

I do not say "white" scholars or "white" writers because of a common tendency amongst diaspora academics to push back against Western racism by presenting a glossier view of their societies of origin than exists in reality. *A Short History of Transmisogyny* by Jules Gil-Peterson still regurgitates the anthropological third-sexing of the hijra, despite its author's desi roots. Gil-Peterson argues that hijras are "much older than the Western concept of gender" and that interpreting them as trans women is a colonial, imperialist act.

This is not a new idea, applied only to trans politics, but rather has been a fixture of debates amongst Western queer people for some time now. A 2021 article by Samuel Huneke for *The Baffler*, entitled *Beyond Gay Imperialism*, talks about the book "The Pink Line" by Mark Gevisser. The book interrogates the idea that the world can be divided into a 'modern', 'progressive', LGBT rights-friendly camp, and "the rest of the world": backwards, uncivilized, barbaric and brutally violent to queer existence.

The article is fascinating because the author discusses the cases of various queer people outside the West: Pasha, who was able to transition through a Moscow gender clinic, or Maha and Amira, a lesbian couple from Cairo. The article goes to great pains to assert that even though non-Western countries may be inhospitable towards queer people, "countries like Egypt and Russia are actually home to complex societies where queer people often find ways to flourish."

The very next line of the article reads: "Many of the individuals Gevisser meets eventually seek asylum in the global North."

I wish to be understanding. I have been told, often, that trying to talk about conservatism, patriarchy, and anti-queer sentiment outside the West is inherently a colonial and racist exercise. Frankly, if Westerners tell me that they are incapable of talking about patriarchy or conservatism outside the West without regressing into frothing, genocidal racists, I'll believe them. Most of them certainly seem incapable of nuance.

However, it does no one any good to attempt to construct a Western fantasy of the rest of the world, and then cite that as an affirmative argument for queer existence. I accept that perhaps Westerners —and US-Americans in particular—are simply too trigger-happy to countenance the existence of a non-Western society that doesn't conform to their moral standards of benevolence, and that trying to ask them to hold this truth in their hearts will result in nuclear apocalypse.

But do your best to accept this information without trying to bomb anyone.

Because the fact of the matter is, there is a YouTube video named *Matt Walsh Asks Maasai Tribe "What is a woman?"*. It has 2.1 million views. The answers he gets don't appear to be quoting Butler.

On a final note, there was an article on Jules Gil-Peterson's Substack that I'd been meaning to cite in an essay all year. It is now deleted, and so I won't talk about it at length. However, the essay stated something that has stuck with me ever since I first read it, the words practically seared into my mind.

"I'm sorry to say that the word trans is frequently a misnomer. What you think is gender is really race. And that's the heart of whiteness right there..."

...Is it, really?

ARYAN NATION

"Love jihad" is an Islamophobic conspiracy theory peddled by Hindutva fascists—that is, those who conceive of India as a "Hindu nation". It is a myth that posits that the men of India's Muslim minority are waging a protracted internal "war" against the Hindu Rashtra by targeting Hindu women for marriage (and thereby forcibly converting them). Interfaith marriages—and indeed, marriage outside one's caste or community without the sanction of your family—continues to be a controversial practice in India today, and I suspect that "love jihad" could have been derived from or is related to the idea of "love marriage"—marrying for love rather than marrying the match selected for you by your elders.

Discounting how widespread domestic abuse is amongst Indians of all faiths for the moment, consider how similar this conspiracy is to white-supremacist replacement conspiracies, and charges of immigrants "invading" Western shores to enact "white genocide". In both cases, we observe a hegemonic demographic discussing its women like a resource being pillaged by an out-group, lying or exaggerating events to construe a minority's existence as inherently aggressive and rallying committed ideologues to the cause—which is, of course, repressive violence against an already-persecuted, marginalized community.

No doubt in the modern day there is a great degree of interpenetration between Hindu and white fascists, and between reactionary men of all sorts around the world. Does that mean that "love jihad" is a *white supremacist* conspiracy? Can we classify it as such, when it's a casus belli fabricated by one non-white population against another?

Nor are these tensions in any way modern. The quote at the top of this essay is from 1945. While religious divisions were exacerbated and instrumentalised by the Raj, and sowing division has been a fixture of colonial politics, the tensions were not invented by Western colonizers out of whole cloth.

Let's recall the Red State article on the 'Transgender Breeding Program', which was written to reiterate a trans groomer panic. The rhetoric in that article is very reminiscent of certain myths that surround hijra, their reputation as child-stealers, and the belief that hijra must be presented with alms should they arrive to commemorate a male child's birth, as otherwise they would abduct the baby as compensation. These beliefs were why, on the 22nd July, 2019, a transgender woman in West Bengal was stoned to death on suspicion of being a "child-lifter". Her name is unknown. Proof of her crimes never surfaced.

So much for 'veneration'.

Maybe every single sin that my society has ever committed has whiteness at its heart. Perhaps colonial rule took a formerly perfectly egalitarian nation and fashioned every division its people now struggle under. We can easily check how true this is, but let us suppose for the sake of this argument that we can't.

Even if a non-Western nation was utopia before colonialism, the fact remains—we were colonised.

The fact remains—we have to reckon with what it is, *today. Now.*

And today, many non-Western societies are far, *far* from gender-expansive. As Kyle James Rohrich details in "Human Rights Diplomacy Amidst 'World War LGBT'", many non-Western regimes are happy to call LGBT rights and LGBT advocacy a facet of 'Western imperialism'. Not only is the idea of recognising the rights of queer people considered an "attack on traditional values", but queer people themselves are frequently treated as a threat to the Nation, as victims of 'Western influence' who must now be treated as hostile entities invested in spreading 'Western pro-LGBT propaganda'. Queer people outside the West, then, find ourselves in a double-bind, where our own cultures treat us as invaders, the vanguard of a supposed colonising force that must be expelled, while the luminaries of the Western academy... also say that trans and queer advocacy are an imperialist, colonial imposition on non-Western societies.

I guess Vladimir Putin is a queer theorist!

This rhetoric precisely mirrors how non-Western antifeminists regard women's rights as well. Everything that could possibly be used to advocate for the plight of marginalized people outside the West is colonial and binarist and a CIA plot, so for the comfort of the non-Western patriarch and the Western intellectual alike, women like me just have to eat shit for the foreseeable future, because our oppression isn't important enough, isn't real enough, is too inconvenient for anyone with power or visibility or the barest shred of epistemic authority on our lives!

It's nonsense. It's contradictions layered atop absurdities, all touted in the name of 'decolonialism' and intersectionality, because heaven fucking forfend if a brown woman wants to be freed from both Western racism *and* homegrown patriarchy!

So no, Judith and Jules and Jack and everyone else I don't have room or time to mention. White people did not invent gender. The concept of patrilineality and treating those who can gestate as reproductive chattel is something non-white people are perfectly capable of figuring out on our own. However inconvenient this might be for the simplistic models of the pre-modern, pre-Western, pre-Fall queer-inclusive matriarchy, we do still have to face the fucking facts. Not just because it's *true,* but because the idea of a global feminism has been ground down into the fucking dirt due to the solipsism of theorists who claim to speak for Third World women without ever once considering what life is like for us, while patriarchal rule itself—due to colonialism or otherwise—remains a transnational enterprise.

The panic over falling birthrates is global. The retrenchment of male-supremacy and the spread of incel ideology is global. The instrumentalisation of trans politics as a right-wing wedge is global.

And you can't fight it if you can't even acknowledge that it's not just white people doing it.

I am sorry if I seem bitter. I simply have had to endure this ahistorical prattle for a lifetime now, and I retain little patience for words that should not be taken seriously in the first place making my life harder. In a way, I do understand the fear. The hesitation. How difficult it is to grapple with the idea that perhaps women and queer people have always been reviled, in every place and time.

But I already did the speech about forging a new path even if it's without precedent in the first book. So all I've got today is, wrap the pity party up already. We have shit to fix.

CONCLUSION: NATIONALISM WITHOUT BORDERS

My best friend met a Chinese butch at the local dyke bar the other day. There was a bit of a language barrier, but they were able to spend a pleasant evening drinking together, for the most part. They exchanged the usual pleasantries before getting into the more personal things. The butch told my friend about how her parents were accepting of her lesbianism.

That's good, you might say, and my friend did in fact say.

To which the butch nodded, before she sighed and talked about how her mother still expected her to have kids. "Yes, fine, be a lesbian," said her mother, "but you can't be childless. You still owe me grandkids."

Owe me grandkids.

White trans people don't experience racism, if you're still wondering. It's just that there are many roads that lead to the same destination: of un-personing, of being decreed unworthy of or unable to further the Nation's goals. A white trans person and a cis person of color in the West both can wield certain weapons against each other, but which weapon will be most effective depends heavily on context, on the conditions under which they meet and on the nature of their conflict. None of us is immune to reaction, or from benefiting from the reactionary systems that seek to turn us into nothing more than instruments of the ruling-class.

That's a less comfortable answer than an absolute ranking of privilege points, I know. Too fucking bad. It's realistic.

The principles of Nationalism are international in two ways. Firstly, in the sense that Nation-building has been one of our oldest misadventures. The desperate need to know who is *one of ours* and who will have your back, morphing into the violent tribalism that continues to haunt our species to this day.

Secondly, in the sense that reactionaries, as Nationalist as they may be, favor the flow of their ideology across borders, tariff-free. Hindutva fascists are in conversation with white supremacists who are in conversation with Israeli settlers and Russian ethnonationalists and religious fundamentalists, and so on and on and on.

The global resurgence of fascism is deeply rooted in the politics of male grievance. The libidinal masculinism of Silicon Valley nouveau riche clowns meeting the traditional fetishism of the zealous preacher and even the gendered anxieties of the young 20-something who desperately wants to get laid and mourns a world where he'd be guaranteed a wife and a family without putting any effort in. It is a response to the idea that women and queer people have a right to exist as equal to men, to be recognised as fully human instead of mere fodder for men's sexual appetites.

We need to recognise it as such.

It is just as farcical to say that feminism is a solely Western fixation as it is to say that European colonists invented patriarchy. Even if the reactionary tendencies amongst those who call themselves feminists must be purged, even if there is yet to be reckoning with the Western tendency to silence non-Western voices, and even if concepts like feminism and gender liberation and queerness and transfemininity are *called different things in different languages*, we still need to recognise how indispensable, how crucial, how central to the fight against tyranny a global feminist consciousness is.

Because there is already a global brotherhood, and we can either keep up with it or submit to its demands.

So let us please approach the topic of gender-liberation with nuance, but without lapsing into antifeminist myths, and without diminishing the relevance of gender-oppression to every struggle. Because what you call race and queerness and disability may or may not have preceded gender, but they are all certainly inseparable from the questions of reproductive control, reproductive value and reproductive fitness that every Nationalist regime seeks to answer. Thirty years of post-feminist bullshit has been enough, and perhaps even too much.

We do not have the luxury of ignoring gender anymore.

5

THE COLONIALITY OF GENDER STUDIES, OR: WHAT IS A NOT-WOMAN?

"KNOWLEDGE IS WEALTH": THE IMPORTANCE OF EDUCATION IN INDIAN SOCIETY

Indians are all taught the story of Eklavya. In the *Mahabharat*, Eklavya was an ordinary boy of prodigious talent, an archer so skilled with no formal training that he shocked even the royal princes' tutor, Dronacharya. He was impassioned, deferential, and respectful, and all he wanted was the honor of Dronacharya's tutelage, under whom he would no doubt flourish.

This presented the legendary *guru* Dronacharya with a dilemma. Yes, Eklavya was an ideal pupil and had passed all of his tests, following every established tradition in his quest for mentorship. Yet Dronacharya's duty was to his royal charges first and foremost, and more selfishly, to Arjun, the most talented of the princes and

Dronacharya's favorite student. Now duty-bound to grant Eklavya's boon, Dronacharya resorted to a morally dubious solution that was still entirely in keeping with our culture's values (or *sanskaar*): he asked Eklavya, as his loyal pupil, to grant *gurudakshina*—a gift to one's teacher—and demand that Eklavya cut off and present his right thumb.

Eklavya, of course, did so without hesitation.

Though the *pundits* debate the sagacity of Dronacharya's actions to this day, especially in the context of how even this small incident held untold ramification for the coming war of succession, we all understand that as students, we owe our teachers—whom we still refer to as *guru*—everything. They are the ones through which we access the most sacred wealth: knowledge itself, a commodity whose indispensability is no better illustrated than by noting that Saraswati and Laxmi are aspects of the same mother goddess. Some believe that our duty to our teachers transcends even that which we owe our parents.

Which has never stopped anyone from passing notes in class, of course.

After all, you can tell children whatever stories you like, but you can't make them pay attention if they don't want to.

We mostly call our teachers "Sir" and "Madam" nowadays, by the way. I don't really have statistics on that, and I haven't exactly checked, but I'm from India. You can take my word for it.

Right?

WESTERN FEMINISM AND THE "THIRD WORLD WOMAN"

Readers of *Trans/Rad/Fem* are no doubt already familiar with the

Western academy's tenuous relationship to the empirical reality of cultures and social structures outside the West. In a discursive landscape that had yet to grapple with the intersections at which multiply-marginalized women were made illegible—leave alone questions of "epistemic injustice"—the "Third World Woman" was initially fashioned as a convenient rhetorical device, tailor-made to prop up ideologies of Western superiority.

The "Third World Woman" was, of course, entirely bereft of both voice and agency, a silent fetish who could only ever be spoken *for*, never spoken *to*. Much ink was spilled on the pronounced and acute state of her abjection: her illiteracy, her jealously-guarded chastity, the total ownership that her father or husband exercised over her, usually exemplified by that most dreaded of garments, the *veil*. Through her, the Western feminist could exalt her own state of liberty, autonomy, and ability to think, read, organize, and agitate—*especially* on behalf of the Western colonial-states, of course. For did not the "Third World Woman", by dint of her very existence, show us all why the West *was*, indeed, Enlightened?

What manner of society did not even allow its women to propagandize for it?

This is the climate that Chandra Talpade Mohanty sought to deconstruct in her paper, *Under Western Eyes*, published in 1984. Here, Mohanty strenuously argues against the prevailing orthodoxies plaguing feminist discourses of the time that flattened, homogenized, and frankly exoticized the "Third World". She pointed out how the complexities and contradictions of Third World existence were entirely erased by these simplistic narratives, and that actual living, breathing women in the Third World did not all suffer a totalizing, uniform abjection. The Third World contained affluent and impoverished women, upper and lower caste women, women of hegemonic and marginalized faiths in theocracies—in short, women whose lives were textured by the multiplicities of their own cultures and states. They did not exist solely for Western aggrandizement, defined by a singular story of suffering that rendered them monolithic and monomythic.

In short, Mohanty was making an argument for *epistemic justice*— for engaging with the complexity of women's oppression in the Third World, and acknowledging that there was no all-encompassing "Third World Womanhood" that rendered them all subject to the same oppression or aligned their interests wholly. The well-off housewife had only so much in common with her live-in maid, after all. It was effectively an argument to afford Third World women the same degree of nuance as Western feminists (sometimes) afforded women in the West, acknowledging and being cognizant of internal disputes and differing goals.

Arguably, this erasure of nuance and the particularities of multiply-marginalized women's lives has been the *central* feminist failure since at least Friedan, if not before. Any feminist movement—wherever it might be located—risks overemphasizing the concerns of the hegemonic demographic, asking the most vulnerable to be the most patient and to put their specific, "lesser" concerns aside for the sake of feminist cohesion and solidarity. From Rich to Mohanty to Crenshaw to Feinberg to Serano, feminism's history could well be succinctly summarized as, "Aren't you forgetting someone?"

For the "Third World woman", this concern is only heightened by the Western academy's privileging of its own perspectives, its own histories, and most of all its own epistemologies. To make herself legible at all, the "Third World woman" has to acquiesce to the West's framing, to use its language, its methodologies, to try to define herself in the realm of its existing ideas and conceptions and assumptions of her life and people. Imagine what it would take for her to be understood on her own terms, as a subject—a *person* shaped by a non-Western society with its own regimes and organization and structures of power.

Could it even be done?

According to Maria Lugones, the name most associated with 'decolonial feminism', we should damn well try.

"DECOLONIZING GENDER"

In 2007, Maria Lugones published *Heterosexualism and the Colonial/Modern Gender System*. She builds on Anibal Quijano's notion of the *coloniality of power*—briefly, the idea that the structuring of precolonial societies by colonizing powers continues to affect and structure those societies post-colonization—to define and discuss a concept she calls the *coloniality of gender*. Lugones draws on the work of Oyèrónké Oyěwùmí, Paula Gunn Allen, and other scholars to illustrate that prior to colonialism, non-Western societies were not in fact organized along hierarchy of binary gender.

"The reason to historicize gender formation is that without this history, we keep on centering our analysis on the patriarchy; that is, on a *binary, hierarchical, oppressive gender formation* that rests on male supremacy without any clear understanding of the mechanisms by which heterosexuality, capitalism, and racial classification are impossible to understand apart from each other. *The heterosexualist patriarchy has been an ahistorical framework of analysis.*" [Emphasis mine.]

Her primary source in the paper is Oyěwùmí's *The Invention of Women*, a book published in 1997 that discusses Yoruba society and gender. Oyěwùmí argues that gender was simply not an organizing principle of precolonial Yoruba society and that to view Yoruba society through this Eurocentric lens of binary and hierarchical gender is in fact to try and fit an ungendered society into a Western mold. In fact, the introduction of gender to precolonial societies is in and of itself a tool of Western domination, to subsume local epistemologies and ways of being. She says:

"The emergence of women as an identifiable category, defined by their anatomy and subordinated to men in all situations, resulted, in part, from the imposition of a patriarchal colonial state. For females, colonization was a twofold process of racial inferiorization and gender subordination. *The creation of 'women' as a category was one of the very first accomplishments of the colonial state.*" [Emphasis mine.]

Lugones and Oyěwùmí are arguing, then, that colonization was the genesis of gender in precolonial societies that had more egalitarian relations between the sexes. As such, *gender* and *race* were inseparable concepts, themselves interlinked with *colonial domination* and *capitalism*, as coterminous systems of power constructed to uphold the myth of Western superiority and secure Western-supremacy. At various points in the essay, Lugones refers to the establishment of patriarchy in precolonial societies as a betrayal, a case of collaboration between the males of a non-Western society and colonizing Western powers.

She also cites Michael J. Horswell, who discusses alternative understandings of gender and sexuality in Andean cultures and analyses his use of the term... "third gender".

Fascinating.

While neither Lugones nor Oyěwùmí are trans scholars or strictly talking about trans people, their ideas have proved to be influential beyond their own disciplines. Many discourses in feminist, queer and trans studies draw directly from the concepts established in this paper and its interpretation of Oyěwùmí's text to discuss the potential and possibility of queer histories and trans acceptance in precolonial times. In that sense, Lugones' concept of the coloniality of gender unites a variety of disparate struggles and invites us to imagine worlds free of Western systems of domination that precede our own.

But is it... you know... true?

Let's consider this paper more generally before focusing on the specifics. *Non-Western society* is a breathtakingly broad category. Singular non-Western countries that exist today are themselves constructions that haphazardly aggregate masses of cultures, hierarchies, peoples, languages, institutions, systems, religions, and histories into a supposedly shared national identity. To make a statement that is both this broad and this definitive about *every non-Western society* would require a very high threshold of evidence, one that these selfsame scholars insist the assertion that "patriarchy is a transcultural phenomenon" does not meet! So to claim that the very opposite is true about Argentina and also India and also China and also Nigeria and also Ukraine, and so on, is both bold and more than a little homogenizing.

Is it not in and of itself an act of colonial Western epistemology to make this statement about *all non-Western societies*? It is arguable whether Lugones and Oyěwùmí make such a strong claim, but the circulation of their ideas and especially their reproduction in queer and feminist discourses regularly do.

There is furthermore the issue of *colonialism* being treated as a singular process or system, without accounting for how different societies experienced colonial violence differently. The indigenous genocide that is the foundation for the United States' settler-colonial order involved near-total levels of epistemicide and erasure in the process of usurpation, but by contrast the colonial relationship between India and

England was not *settler-colonial*. It was a much more extractive relationship, with India being treated as a site of wealth to loot (and today, as a site of cheap labor to exploit), but there was nowhere near as holistic an attempt to supplant and replace India's societies on India's lands. Transform and disrupt them to reorient them towards the purposes of extractivist colonialism and the hollowing out of both land and people? Almost certainly. But while Indian history will likely always be filtered through a degree of Anglophonic and colonial translation and interpretation... there's still a lot of Indian history, and Chinese history, and other histories that are far less (allegedly) unknowable and ambiguous than the histories destroyed by Native genocide.

Despite these clear material differences, Western discourses on the violence of colonialism—ironically—*even discount and homogenize non-Western perspectives on colonial violence.*

Once more, this principally occurs in queer and feminist discourses that do not much care to differentiate between colonialism as a process of usurpation and replacement, or colonialism as a process of displacement and enslavement, or colonialism as a process of wealth extraction and pillaging. While these processes may look broadly similar and no doubt have large degrees of overlap, the distinction is important to make, especially when describing non-Western people's relationship to their own precolonial understandings.

So on a very basic, almost tautological level, this is not a true claim in the way it is usually deployed—broad, totalizing, and homogenizing. If the claim that patriarchy is both transhistorically and transculturally extant does not meet evidentiary standards, then these claims about non-patriarchal precolonial societies fall much, much further short.

But also... are the claims even true about Yoruba society *specifically* ?

CONSTRUCTING A NON-GENDERED SOCIETY

There's an interesting paper I came across during the process of research, published in 2024 in the journal of feminist philosophy *Hypatia*. The following is a snippet from the abstract of *Sexual Difference and Decolonization: Oyěwumɪ and Irigaray in Dialogue about Western Culture*:

"In this article we aim to show the potential of cross-continental dialogues for a decolonizing feminism. We relate the work of one of the major critics of the Western metaphysical patriarchal order, Luce Irigaray, to the critique of the colonial/modern gender system by the Nigerian feminist scholar Oyèrónkẹ́ Oyěwùmí. *Oyěwùmí's work is often rejected based on the argument that it is empirically wrong.* ..." [Emphasis mine.]

Oh, dear.

Oyěwùmí's argument in *The Invention of Women* about gender not being a relevant organizational factor in precolonial Yoruba society rests on three prongs. The first is a linguistic argument, centering on the notion that Yoruba language is less gendered than—let's say English, even though Oyěwùmí talks about 'Western' and 'Eurocentric' linguistic understandings as though they're all reducible to the English understanding. The second is the assertion that Yoruba society is organized by *seniority*, not gender. The third is that statistics are fake and Western. On page 77:

"Odds are the supreme language of statistics speaks to the Western obsession with measurement and the *preoccupation with 'evidence that we can see.'*" [Emphasis mine.]

And on page 110:

"My discussion of statistical categoricalism in the previous chapter dealt with the issue of whether a legitimate argument can be made about the statistical prevalence of anafemales in a particular trade. *Suffice it to say here that the question of gender and numbers does not arise from the [Oyo] frame of reference;* it, of course, fits in very well with the Western bio-logic framework." [Emphasis mine.]

The crux of Oyěwùmí's argument here is that statistical analyses of, for example, the number of women and men in particular trades to gauge how gendered the trade is and whether women are under-represented, is not a relevant lens through which to view Yoruba society, and in fact such statistical analyses effectively create the gendered reality they wish to observe. By, well, observing how many men or women are present in particular arenas or domains. Allegedly, statisticians must first prove that "man" and "woman" are meaningful categories in Yoruba society before trying to measure how gendered specific aspects of Yoruba society are.

This is less an argument and more a circular reasoning for why Oyěwùmí's claims about gender not being a meaningful social organizing category ought to be treated as unfalsifiable. If Yoruba society is not preoccupied with gender, but *empirical observations* do not show that men and women are roughly evenly distributed across a cross-section of professions or classes, then perhaps gender *is* a determining factor in some way. That is implied by the observation.

There is one more thing Oyěwùmí says about statistics. She alleges that by observing, say, a disproportionate number of men in a field or trade, those doing the analysis downplay and dismiss the *exceptions*, the women who are also present but outnumbered. Keep that in mind for later.

Let's return to the linguistic argument. Oyěwùmí holds that the

Yoruba categories *obinrin* and *okunrin* are translated by Western researchers, who "always find gender when they look for it", as 'female/woman' and 'male/man' respectively. According to Oyěwùmí, this is a mistranslation: "These categories are neither binarily opposed nor hierarchical." Instead, the terms *obinrin* and *okunrin* merely indicate "anatomic distinction" and insists that they are better translated as " *anatomical* female" and "*anatomical* male", or "anafemale" and "anamale" for short.

...So that's... interesting...

Perhaps a transfeminine perspective here might be invaluable. Leaving aside the sleight of hand in including the word 'female' alongside 'woman' when asserting that *obinrin* is a mistranslation, as though 'female' does not have principally anatomic connotations, the idea that the word 'woman' is first and foremost regarded by most Westerners—even most Western researchers and scholars—as a *social* and not *anatomical* or *biologically-essentialist* category is giving the West far, far too much credit! You need only look at the X feed of a certain wizard kidlit author and their disciples to disabuse yourself of the notion that Western linguistic understandings of gender encode and communicate a primarily social hierarchy—that assumes feminist discourses to be far, far more widespread than they actually are!

But also... is the idea that Yoruba language encodes and communicates anatomical differences without gendered connotations actually, you know... true?

BIBI BAKARE-YUSUF'S *YORUBAS DON'T DO GENDER: A CRITICAL REVIEW* (2000)

Bibi Bakare-Yusuf is a Nigerian academic and writer who has studied communication, anthropology and gender studies abroad. Her work is not as well known as Oyěwùmí's for reasons that will become clear later, and in 2000 she published a critical review of *The Invention of Women*.

"Recently, some African scholars have begun to question the explanatory power of gender in African societies. This challenge came out of the desire to produce concepts grounded in African thought and everyday lived realities. These scholars hope that by focusing on an African episteme they will avoid any dependency on European theoretical paradigms and therefore eschew what Babalola Olabiyi Yai (1999) has called 'dubious universals' and 'intransitive discourses'."

Bakare-Yusuf describes Oyěwùmí's methodology as problematic and her understanding of both language and the Yoruba system of seniority as simplistic and naive. She reminds us that language is also an evolving, living thing, that the same word can carry different meanings and connotations even between different places during the same era, and that by purporting to uncover a "pure essence" of Yoruba language free of gendered implications, Oyěwùmí effectively situates it out of history, time, and the forces of change. Yet it is the question of 'seniority not gender' that proves to be most illustrative of Oyěwùmí's approach and priors:

"The essential pitfall of her account of power, whether that of seniority in Yorubaland or gender distinction in the west, is that a particular variable of power is the same everywhere in isolation from any other form of enablement or constraint. One can readily concede that Oyewumi is right to argue that seniority is the dominant language of power in Yoruba culture. However, she is wrong to conclude that seniority is the only form of power relationship and that it operates outside of or in relation to other forms of hierarchy."

It's almost like distinct forms of power can co-exist... and impact the same person simultaneously... in a sort of *overlap*, or say, *intersection*...

Bakare-Yusuf further stresses that Oyěwùmí's reductive reading of power relations in Yoruba culture preclude her from understanding that seniority is oftentimes invoked as a cover for other forms of inequality or power imbalance:

"*The vocabulary of seniority often becomes the very form in which sexual abuse, familial (especially for the aya/wife in a lineage) and symbolic violence is couched.* Her refusal to complicate or interrogate the workings of power is even more alarming giving the virulent abuse of power in the teacher-student relationship in the Nigerian education system that often goes unchallenged by the victim because they are loathe to challenge the abuser in the name of 'disrespecting their senior' . .... *Seniority in the Yoruba context is therefore often a ruse for other forms of power. However, because Oyěwùmí wants seniority to stand alone as the dominant mode of power in the Yoruba social system,* she simply cannot recognise blurred reality for what it is. *She therefore must avoid all work done by feminists and social theorists that stresses the complex interdependency* of one form of power upon another and the ways in which one explicitly manifested (and respected!) power often *conceals other more insidious ones.*" [Emphasis mine.]

Speaking from the Indian context, I want to point out that the idea of seniority as a form of social power relations, especially within joint and extended families, is hardly exclusive to Yoruba culture—nor is it exactly decoupled from gender relations! Because the source of an elder's authority within a family structure is as much about their role as a progenitor to whom their children and children's families owe deference, which is very much a form of reproductive logic!

There's also the fact that Oyěwùmí notes in the book that it is customary for Yoruba women to relocate to their husbands' households after marriage, which instantly removes them from their old hierarchical position and places them on the bottom of a new one as the most recent entrant, on the same level as newborn infants. She then does not interrogate this observation at all.

Finally, on the subject of gender-neutrality predicated on non-gendered language, Bakare-Yusuf observes:

"For Oyěwùmí, there are no barriers to obinrin's activities in relation to okunrin. That is, the biological fact of being female does not interrupt or determine in any way (beyond the obvious fact of reproduction) the social perceptions of bodies. It is this *alleged gender neutrality* that affords ana-females in the Yoruba context the level of freedom and capacity that they enjoy. *However, just because gender difference is not inscribed within discourse or marked within language doesn't mean that it is entirely absent in social reality.* There is often a gap between what happens in law and social reality. It is precisely by *not making a distinction between language and reality* that Oyěwùmí is able to elide this possibility and assume that Yoruba women have the same power as men in their lineage." [Emphasis mine.]

It's a shame that statistics are too Western to give us any insight into the gendered reality of Yoruba society.

Given the way that Oyěwùmí recoils from empiricism, in addition to the licenses she takes in interpreting the West as distinct from Yoruba society in ways it likely isn't, it is perhaps fair to conclude that her reasoning is motivated by her conclusion rather than the other way around. Oyěwùmí wants to make these assertions about Yoruba society, despite the fact that, per Bakare-Yusuf, the wives of the household typically have food-preparation and child-rearing responsibilities in a way that "male wives" (men who relocate to their wives' household instead of the inverse) simply do not. Oyěwùmí is attached to the idea that exceptions to the rule mean that one cannot make gendered assertions about Yoruba culture, and relies on those exceptions heavily in her reasoning, but as Bakare-Yusuf says:

"While one can sympathise with the therapeutic value motivating Oyewumi's desire to uncover a pre-colonial, harmonious, ungendered history, the evidence she uses to support her argument simply does not stand up to scrutiny. We cannot simply use the experience of princesses and privileged women to evaluate the position and experience of most women in society."

Here, I must apologize to my readers for withholding crucial context that would enable them to read this declaration from Bakare-Yusuf with the appropriate tone. You see, in the very Preface of *The Invention of Women*, Oyěwùmí explains that she was born into a large family, and in 1973 her father ascended the throne to become the *Soun* of Ogbomoso.

She also says that she is indebted to her siblings, parents, and "the many mothers and fathers in the palace" for their contributions to her many years of research.

Now, far be it for me to question whether the perspective of a royal family can be drawn upon to accurately portray what life is like for everyday men and women, which would imply that Oyěwùmí's assertions about gender cannot even be applied to *all of Yoruba society*. Let's entertain the idea that the existence of influential and affluent women necessarily implies that those women's cultures cannot be held to be patriarchal. Applying this logic would lead one to necessarily conclude that England under Queen Victoria was a non-gendered, non-patriarchal society.

You know, the Victorian England that was a colonial power. The one that is charged by scholars of various disciplines as having introduced the 'colonial' and hierarchical gender binary to non-Western societies. I suppose that England is exonerated of these charges and we have to look elsewhere for the True Source of Evil from which patriarchy emerged. Perhaps Middle-Earth.

Of course, there is also the matter of Oyěwùmí's other opinions on gender, including her views on the 'Western' practice of homosexuality. In 2004, Oyěwùmí edited an anthology entitled *African Women and Feminism: Reflecting on the Politics of Sisterhood*. The second chapter, written by her, contains the following:

"The insistence on the part of Western women to *label what African women call female circumcision* 'mutilation' was the first visible sign of deep divisions between them and many of their African counterparts ... A number of other African institutions that Westerners view as barbaric include *arranged marriages, levirate, and* **child betrothal**. These practices are *misrepresented as misogynistic* and *not placed in their cultural and social contexts* that would allow Westerners to discern their meaning from the perspective of African societies."

Okay. We really need to talk about this trick.

Recall, if you will, Chandra Talpade Mohanty and *Under Western Eyes*. Mohanty cautions against the flattening and homogenization of complex systems and societies outside the West—*just as Oyěwùmí did here*, referring to a notion of "African societies" that uniformly accept practices like FGM and *child betrothal* more neutrally than the also-homogenized specter of hysterical "Western women" do. As if there are no African women or African movements or African feminisms opposing these practices. As if the perspectives of the most conservative, visible, affluent and well-connected elements of a non-Western society must be granted epistemic authority enough for all society, including the elements of society they do not meaningfully share many interests with!

Oyěwùmí here is not concerned with the unvarnished truth, the complexities of non-Western systems of oppression, and certainly not with feminism of any kind. The clue is in the word *barbaric*, which belies a preoccupation with how her society and people are *perceived* by the West. Her statements about gender and seniority and misogyny must all be considered with the context that she occupies a certain place in her society that makes her more preoccupied with its image than whether its people truly accept all its traditions and customs. Her work represents the apotheosis of academic discourse between the racism of the West and the classism of the upper-crust of non-Westerners.

It is this fixation on image that compels Oyěwùmí to engage in a strange dialogue with the works of Alice Walker, within this same anthology. Oyěwùmí takes issue with Walker's idea that West African societies had "culturally sanctioned and institutionalized forms of lesbianism", accusing Black feminists of speaking over African perspectives and applying contemporary Western discourses of sexuality onto indigenous African contexts.

So, you know, the scholar whose work has most trickled down into queer scholarship that claims a pre-patriarchal and queer-inclusive precolonial paradigm is one whose idea of "non-gendered" society cannot even countenance the prevalence or acceptance of lesbianism.

Cool!

WESTERNERS SEEM TO BE REALLY FUCKING GULLIBLE

Did you believe the things I said about Indian society in the very first section of this essay? You really shouldn't have. I can spin a pretty story about Hindu values and the deference we owe our teachers, but India is not a purely Hindu country, nor does its Hindu population necessarily live lives guided by the teachings of an ancient epic it would take aeons to read.

Also, the story of Eklavya is more about caste than anything else, because Eklavya was a lower-caste boy who tried to reach above his station, and was dealt with accordingly.

This is going to be the least rigorous part of this piece, because I'm kind of just fed up. Judith Butler in *Who's Afraid of Gender?* talks about how authoritarians in the West live in a 'phantasm', a reality of their own making that they have retreated into because actual reality challenges and complicates their understandings of power, hierarchy, and how the world 'should' be. Butler was wrong.

Because I'm pretty sure it's not just authoritarians.

The West's relationship to the Third World remains a deeply orientalist one. Even amongst those who are more aware of social ills—perhaps *especially* amongst such people—the idea that an entire unfamiliar world exists past colonized borders is incredibly enticing. What can these strange and faraway people and places that I know very little about and refuse to look at objectively teach me about a better, less rigid, less *Western* way of life? Maybe I should listen to this charlatan who is trying to push a very particular narrative? It would be racist of me not to, right?

Well, folks, swallowing whatever bullshit someone with a particular outlook and interests sells you isn't exactly egalitarian and decolonial.

This is where I'd caution folks to be critical about my work too, but I don't seem to need to bother. People who are very attached to the fictions and fabrications I have zero patience for somehow managed to find the ability to be nuanced about *my* life and point of view, and constantly invent novel ways to call me 'white' or 'Western', ascribing to me a level of privilege and subjecting me to a level of scrutiny that actual princesses escape. People are plenty skeptical about what I write, don't you worry, because the bedtime stories are more important than coming to terms with just how fucking complicated life is everywhere and just how much conservative, reactionary, and nationalist logic pervades thinking all over the world.

The only purpose I can ascribe to this level of attachment to trumped-up and difficult to substantiate visions of precolonial life is a desire for a far simpler world than the one that actually exists, where solidarity is not impossible but requires a hell of a lot of work across movements, cultures and interests. What if we could get everyone on board with slaying The One Dragon Responsible For All Evil? What if we could cast the One Ring of Whiteness into the fires of Mount Decolonize? What if we could crawl back into the prelapsarian womb that I was untimely ripped from and to which I can definitely, definitely return? Wouldn't that be nice?

It would, but it's not a particularly useful or productive or predictive model of the world, so fucking deal.

Worst of all, I genuinely cannot envision how it would matter even if this idealist precolonial utopia was real. Let's just believe everything for a moment. Let's allow that in the past—the very recent past, even! —all societies outside the West were paradises where trans people were revered and queer people were accepted and men actually loved the women they fucked. Then 200-400 years ago, The White Nation attacked and plunged us into this centuries-long dystopia.

So fucking what?

Can we roll the world back to an earlier version on git? Can we go up to the manager of Patriarchy and Imperialism and say, "Excuse me sir, we *used* to exist in harmony and peace. Doesn't exploiting us now make you feel bad?"

Even Lugones admits that this model of history and colonial relations condemns non-Western men as traitors and turncoats, as scum who overthrew the harmony of their peaceful society in exchange for property rights over women! If it were all true, we would still have to deal with that, to contend that systems of domination and power and gender hold a certain appeal to those who are granted certain benefits. We would still have to analyze these systems as having incentives, as having an appeal for those who aren't on the absolute bottom rung. Keep looking into and interpreting our past, and believe in the fairy tale if you like, but that doesn't actually change what must be done today and now.

And frankly, I don't even think the story is that inspiring. I think the fact that despite the lack of historical precedence women and trans people and queer people have still fought for and secured rights, that we are sitting here envisioning and fighting for better worlds, is a hell of a lot more inspiring than the idea that I must seek out a lost paradise. It is, frankly, tantamount to spitting on the memories of those who come before us and everything they fought for.

Because I am proud of my foremothers, and I don't understand why more of us aren't.

I may be many things, but I am most certainly a woman. Neither my transness nor my brownness nor my lesbianism nor anything else about me makes me less of one. I am regarded as reproductive offal and a valid target of sexual violence under patriarchy. I fight to change that.

Do you?

6

NO COUNTRY FOR NON-MEN: THE HONOR CULTURE OF DIASPORA FEMINISTS

INTRODUCTION: DO DESI WOMEN DREAM OF BEATING UP WEDDINGS?

Trans/Rad/Fem is not my first book.

When I began writing, I started off as an author of lesbian romance. The first book I wrote and published is a much lesser-known Bollywood-inspired desi lesbian romance named *Dulhaniyaa* (which means 'bride', and is a rather explicit nod to perhaps the most famous Bollywood romance of all time: *Dilwaale Dulhaniyaa Le Jayenge*, or 'Lovers Will Steal The Bride Away'). Growing up, I lacked the language to express why I connected so much with flamboyant, campy musicals about star-crossed lovers whose families opposed their union, and did not understand until much later why I was disturbed by how distressingly heterosexual these movies always were.

So, I wrote *Dulhaniyaa*. Esha, an NRI, gives up on art school and returns to India to marry the man her family picked out for her. Esha is a lesbian, but her heart is broken, and unable to see any way out of what's expected of her, she does what many women in her position do —gives in. She doesn't expect that her dance instructor, hired to help her perform a choreographed number at her own wedding, will be someone she slowly falls in love with. By the end of the book, Esha must choose between accepting her family's wishes and her own happiness.

In a sense, *Dulhaniyaa* is my attempt to write out the Bollywood story I never thought I'd get to see. Two lesbian leads fighting to be together in the face of the all-encompassing patriarchy of India. It's a short novel, barely longer than a novella, and tries to capture as much of Bollywood's charm as is possible in a textual medium, complete with musical numbers and costume changes and physics-defying motorcycle chases. And while *Dulhaniyaa*'s modest success is greatly overshadowed by *Trans/Rad/Fem*'s performance, it still holds a special place in my heart as the Bollywood story where the queer subtext of separation and familial disapproval gets to just... be text. The Bollywood story that I wrote because I'll never be able to watch it.

Or so I thought, until I came across Nida Manzoor's 2023 masterpiece, *Polite Society*.

How do I explain *Polite Society*? Officially, it's described as a 'martial-arts action-comedy' when in fact it is a radical feminist horror movie, though explaining why counts as spoilers. (Of which there will be many in this essay.) It is a story about the Khan sisters, Ria and Lena, and how their sisterhood is put to the test by patriarchy's relentless attempts to steal women away from each other. Ria, the younger of the two, wants to be a stuntwoman after school, while Lena failed out of art school and has moved back home. They are both struggling with the strict demands that their South Asian parents, the wider UK South Asian community, and a patriarchal world at large makes of women—particularly non-white, *creative* women—like them.

While *Polite Society* is written from the perspective of second-generation Muslim immigrant characters, I feel confident asserting that South Asian women of a variety of backgrounds will find it relatable. The relentless parental and specifically maternal pressure to get married and start a family, the way community elders judge unmarried and putatively 'directionless' young women, and the enduring love of and homages to Bollywood cinema make it a rather transcendent and pertinent film. Exhausted and embittered and burned out, Lena makes a choice that many women in her position have made: to give in. Lena attends a soirée thrown by an affluent member of the community trying to find suitable matches for her precious baby boy. Lena ends up being shortlisted as the ideal vessel for his seed, and accepts an offer of marriage.

Young, naive and idealistic Ria sees this as a betrayal—not of her, but of Lena's authentic self. There is a charged, emotional scene where Lena and Ria, screaming at the top of their lungs and punching each other through their bedroom walls, have an argument best summed up as "This isn't you!" v/s "Yes, it is!" The action and musical set pieces in *Polite Society*, like the action and dance numbers in Bollywood, are a way to literalise furious, intense exchanges, where every word feels like a punch to the gut—so why not visually depict it as such?

"I'm not good enough!" Lena screams, and breaks both her and Ria's heart.

This puts Ria in the position usually reserved for male love interests: refusing to accept the female lead's nuptials and resolving to do whatever it takes to call it off. She snoops on the groom, tries to plant evidence of him cheating, and alienates both family and friends in her out-of-control attempts to go against even Lena's explicitly stated wishes. Eventually, Ria concedes the error of her ways and goes to Lena's future mother-in-law to apologise. She learns a valuable lesson about not clinging to her immature view of the world, growing up, and accepting the people who will be her new family.

Or she *would*, if she didn't uncover a secret lab where Lena's future husband analyzed dozens of DNA samples and uterus scans collected from the women who attended the soirée! Lena was selected by the uncomfortably emotionally incestuous mother-son duo for her exceptional fecundity, which makes her the perfect broodmare for cloning her future mother-in-law in a horribly literalised metaphor for the way desi boymoms see their sons and daughter-in-laws as nothing more than an opportunity to vicariously live the lives they were denied.

Surprise! *Polite Society* is actually a sci-fi radfem body horror!

Determined to prevent Lena from becoming nothing more than a womb for her in-laws to exploit (subtle!), Ria enlists the help of her friends in an explosive climax that is a dearly-held wish fulfillment power fantasy of many a South Asian woman: kicking the living daylights out of an entire Indian wedding. Just absolutely going to town on condescending aunties and swarms of relatives you've never met and the loser who doesn't even care about or deserve the woman he's marrying, with a special flying spin-kick reserved for the overbearing mother-in-law.

That is what really struck me the most about *Polite Society*. Nida Manzoor and I have no doubt lived very different lives, and yet I can see everything we both love and abhor—down to shot-for-shot recreations of pivotal moments from *The Matrix*—in her story that's so eerily similar to my own. Nida Manzoor gave me the Bollywood movie I never thought I'd get to see, and even made it unapologetically radfem.

Though... there is that *one* thing.

Ria and Lena were written as sisters, not lovers. This was a very deliberate choice, because *Polite Society* is in conversation with a genre that always centers men. Even the principal antagonist in *Polite Society* isn't really Lena's groom, but her mother-in-law, because the story is unabashedly about women even as it's about patriarchy, commenting on the many, many ways in which women often fail each other.

Is the movie about one woman helping another escape her arranged marriage making a point about the sisterhood we ought to owe each other, by making the character who would usually be the bride's lover into her sister instead? Absolutely.

But it could have just easily been about a woman who loves another woman and tries to save her from succumbing to the patriarchal expectations under whose weight she is being crushed. It might have even taken less work than reworking the trope entirely.

I find myself asking: is a woman any less of a sister when she is a lesbian? Are those of us who do not love men any less capable of understanding the endless, soul-destroying demands to let yourself be exploited by them? As someone intimately familiar with the stories Manzoor is both paying homage to and critiquing, I can't help but notice the quiet discomfort with queerness in the contours of the narrative. *Polite Society* remains haunted by battles past and present, waged on the topic of which women belong in feminist movements—non-white, lesbian, trans, colonised, impoverished, and others.

I guess I'm still waiting for my perfect Bollywood movie. I harbor no hopes of *Dulhaniyaa* ever being adapted to the silver screen, but there's more and more queer creatives every day. Maybe I'll still get my wish. Maybe I won't even have to wait that long. I choose to be optimistic.

PART ONE: "IS 'HONOR-KILLING' A RACIST TERM?"

To Specify or Single Out: Should We Use The Term 'Honor Killing'? by Rochelle L. Terman was published in 2010, in the *Muslim World Journal of Human Rights*. It explores the phenomenon of 'honor killings', which is the name given to specific cases of femicide that occur within certain ethnic groups. Principally, the article discusses the differing attitudes towards the term between various women's groups, and asks whether the use of this specific term serves only to racially mark certain communities as "particularly patriarchal", or "backwards", or worthy of greater scrutiny and surveillance.

The article makes a lot of strange assertions not backed up by the facts it goes over. It asks at length why there needs to be a distinction between 'honor killing' and 'domestic violence', without taking into account the factors that make 'honor killings' unique. Firstly, the text itself concedes are usually carried out by the victim's *premarital* family, not typically by her spouse or in-laws. On page 25:

"It is not enough to return the woman to her family home after a time of 'cooling off' or to send her to the care of relatives; either option puts her in grave harm. Furthermore, in the UK for instance, one in eight honor killings are committed by hit men hired by the family of the victim."

[A note: the term "hit men" strikes me as a bit of a fanciful exaggeration; in the cases where a woman's father, brother or husband does not carry out the killing himself, it is usually done by another male "member of the community".]

Secondly, 'honor killings' are carried out against women who are said to bring "shame" upon the family, usually by violating endogamy and having intimate relations with a man external to her community, or who was not approved by her family. While the communities these femicides occur within condone both IPV and this rationale for femicide—considering these "private, family affairs"—the definitional lethality of 'honor killings' and the particular rationale behind them should give us some cause to distinguish the phenomenon from the broader umbrella of 'domestic violence'.

Terman has a frustrating tendency to obscure important details about the motivations behind these femicides. She talks about how "there has been much feminist political scholarship arguing that women are seen as the main transmitters of social values and the primary boundary-makers of cultural and religious identity", which is a rather long-winded way of saying that it's about controlling women's chastity, modesty, and how they are allowed to present in public. Of the two cases the article covers—Aqsa Parvez and and Aasiya Hassan—Aqsa was killed by her father for not wearing her hijab in public, while Aasiya was beheaded by her husband for getting a restraining order in response to his abuse. In both cases, the matter was one of insubordination, of women who exercised more autonomy than their role as patriarchal property permitted them.

Further, the question of why women's groups are divided on the term 'honor killing' has a fascinating answer. An illuminating snippet from page 22 reads:

"Some minority women's groups who acknowledge that honor killings are a problem among immigrant groups in Europe and North

America and work to combat them are often criticized by various elements. On one hand, they are *vulnerable to attack by conservative forces on the grounds that they represent 'inauthenticity,' 'Westernization,' and 'secularism' for not respecting indigenous honor culture*, particularly if they working on sexuality-related issues and violence against women (Welchman and Hossein 2005:18). Ironically, they are sometimes criticized by progressive or leftist groups *'washing our dirty laundry in public'* (Siddiqui 2005: 274)." [Emphasis mine.]

This is a statement made more damning by the acknowledgement that honor killings are still called 'honor killings' outside the West— that is, even in homeland contexts where there is no Western media element to allegedly weaponise the term in a 'racist' manner. As a matter of fact, the term 'honor killing' is simply a literal translation of what would be the phenomenon's name in various languages, which is predicated on the concept of *izzat*—a word that quite simply (at least in Hindi) means 'honor' or 'respectability', specifically the honor of the family or clan.

It is a social norm rooted entirely in the idea that respectable families are ones who are able to best "control" their daughters and prevent them from being "loose", enforcing modesty culture and refusing to entertain the notions of autonomous sexuality amongst women. A family that fails to control its women in this way—be they wives or daughters—must wipe clean the stain of shame brought upon it by eliminating the errant daughter who dares betray her community and refuses to uphold her duty as her in-group's reproductive property.

That this is acceptable in certain cultures is, indeed, fucked up, regardless of whether or not it makes immigrant communities look bad to Westerners!

The source of the split between women's advocacy groups is then, plainly, about whether we ought to prioritise and bring attention to the actual suffering of non-white women within immigrant communities, or whether we ought to subsume the unique circumstances they suffer under into the broader category of 'domestic violence' in the name of "better PR", or "not making our men and communities look bad"— because expecting men to *not kill their womenfolk* is certainly out of the option, isn't it! Women, as the seat of a nation's future, as the source of a family's honor, who have the power to shame our entire bloodlines but lack the freedom to determine our own futures, must weigh the pros and cons of "keeping our affairs private", swallowing our own blood through broken teeth, or else risk being used as racist, xenophobic propaganda by regimes eager to exploit our suffering as a casus belli against the second-class citizens that comprise our people.

Which way, non-Western woman?

PART TWO: BETWEEN SCYLLA AND CHARYBDIS

We Are Lady Parts is a two-season, 12-episode comedy by Nida Manzoor about an all-female Muslim punk band. Its first season debuted in 2021, and its second concluded the series in 2024.

We open on Amina Hussain, a second-generation immigrant who is trying and failing to find a nice Muslim boy to marry. Her liberal parents are, amusingly, more of a hindrance than a help in this regard, with her checked-out father and bubbly mother prone to oversharing details shattering the careful image of a modest, conservative, and homely woman that Amina is desperately trying to cultivate. The show makes an interesting decision here, choosing to examine the phenomenon of immigrant kids who—usually in response to the xenophobia and racism of their new homes—sometimes embrace the conservative values of their cultures of origin to a greater degree than even their parents. Amina isn't being pressured into an arranged marriage, in contrast to Lena in *Polite Society*, though it is heavily implied she believes asking her parents to find her a suitable match is the only acceptable way for her to express how (bluntly) boy-crazy she is.

The one exception to Amina's halal ways is her love of music: she is a huge fan of Don McLean and teaches underprivileged children how to play guitar. This sets her on a collision course with the titular punk band, *We Are Lady Parts*, who find themselves looking for a lead guitarist.

At the start of the show, the band comprises four members: Bisma, the bassist, who has a husband and child and draws gory comics about period blood; Momtaz, the niqabi band manager; Ayesha, the drummer and only queer member; and Saira, a breathtaking butch vision in oversized flannel and ripped jeans who works as a *butcher*, ha, in her spare time and is the band's lead vocalist and frontwoman and smoldering heartthrob.

I may have a favorite amongst them.

The events of the first season are set in motion when Amina happens across Ayesha's adequate-looking brother handing out audition flyers and agrees to join the band in exchange for a date with him. It's a decision that brings her to her breaking point, as Amina juggles overcoming her stage fright, being rejected after the date, and helping plan her equally-conservative friend's wedding while keeping her double life with *Lady Parts* a secret, phrasing intentional. Though Saira does have a cardboard cutout of a man who makes no impression and evaporates in the sixth episode, never to be seen again, the season is entirely about

Saira's affection and affinity for Amina, to the point that even the cardboard cutout notices.

"I'm just jealous! This Amina clearly has you all hot and bothered."

Much like *Polite Society*, the first season of *We Are Lady Parts* is about sisterhood and the bond between women who find comfort in each others' arms. However, it is also more explicit about exploring the characters' place as *brown* and *Black* women in Western society, and how the pressure to be modest and uphold their community's *honor* clashes with their own desires, freedom, and expression. Ayesha drives an Uber for white men who are racist to her, Saira's mother asks her to remain away from home for as long as Saira clings to gender-nonconformity, and Amina is constantly trying to reconcile the shame she feels at not being a perfect, modest woman with how much she loves being in *Lady Parts*, phrasing intentional. They are all hypervigilant, knowing that they are constantly being judged by their own people and by a xenophobic, Western gaze.

The emotional core of the first season is summed up perfectly by Faiz Ahmed Faiz's poem *Speak*, which Saira dedicates and symbolically gifts to Amina on two occasions. In the face of all the pervasive forces seeking to control you, your voice, and your creative vision, you must...

"*Speak, for your two lips are free. Speak, for your tongue is still your own.*" — Saira to Amina, heterosexually.

Nida Manzoor's art speaks to me because it speaks to experiences that so many of us struggle to name, to speak up about, to see even in art by and about us. She captures that particular feeling of slowly choking on all the contradictory expectations a world that fundamentally does not value brown women places on us, of being trapped between homeland and occident, of having to choose every day between Scylla and Charybdis. It's nerdy, empowering, heartfelt, unapologetically feminist, cringe at times, and all the better for it because it's *sincere*. She brings to life women who share my pain in a way many, many portrayals of people who look like me lack. She, in a word, *gets it*.

Though her work doesn't really explore queer narratives textually, there is still a powerful queer undercurrent to it. Maybe that's because it's difficult to be feminist and make art about loving and valuing women without being at least a little homoerotic, or maybe it's because queer brown women, despite our extra baggage, have a lot in common with non-queer brown women. Shocking, I know. Whether or not it's intentional, Nida Manzoor's work is special and powerful and resonant in a way I hope my own work can someday be.

It's really tempting to end on this effusive, positive note. Everything I've written here is honest and reflects my authentic feelings about a creator whose art is very dear to me. And yet, there's something else that I have to talk about.

Because *We Are Lady Parts* Season One *does* have a textually queer narrative, and it's... something.

SISTER, OUTSIDER

Episode Four of *We Are Lady Parts* introduces us to Zarina, an influencer with over a million followers. Zarina talks about being "by and for women of color" in a cloyingly liberal manner that makes the band members—specifically Ayesha—gag a little, but Momtaz insists that Zarina holds the key to putting *Lady Parts* on the map. She organises a meeting with Zarina, whereupon the previously-unimpressed Ayesha falls in love with her at first sight. This is also the first textual indication of Ayesha's queerness.

Zarina's praise for the band is effusive, and as the editor of a widely-read online publication, she offers to do a feature on *Lady Parts*, which sounds very appealing to Ayesha in particular. The band almost immediately gets a gig through Zarina, though when they arrive at the venue —a pub filled with older, white Englishmen—they have some reservations.

Playing for such a crowd goes about as well as one might expect: they encounter a fair bit of racist, sexist heckling, followed by very little applause. It's still a triumphant moment for the band, however, because Amina finally overcomes her stage fright. While the girls celebrate, the camera zooms in on Zarina, who is busy slipping the bigoted hecklers some cash.

This pivotal exchange answers a burning question that bothered me as soon as the pub scene began: how could people as open-minded as white, British men be compelled to utter misogynistic insults and racially-charged invective? Why, naturally, they were bribed!

The next episode shows Zarina interviewing the band for her feature, though her questions are all highly charged and extremely leading. "Does your husband stop you from working?" she asks Bisma. "Some might say you're doing this for attention," she says of Momtaz's niqab. Ayesha, who Zarina is now dating, does not escape this treatment either, as Zarina pressures her to come out and talk about being a queer, Muslim woman, backing off only when Ayesha firmly draws the line.

When Zarina releases the article, titled *The Bad Girls of Islam*, none of the band members take it well. "*Lady Parts* say 'fuck you' to both their religion and the West", it declares, to everyone's horror. Zarina has twisted their words, portraying them as women who publicly denigrate their own community, and without any regard for their privacy or safety is using them as rage-bait to farm engagement and clicks! How could she possibly have stooped so low as to publicly release the article they had all agreed to be interviewed for, hoping for more eyes on their music? While insinuating that four women in a punk band had anything negative to say about their conservative up-bringings?

This heinous betrayal nearly breaks the band apart. Amina recalls her more fundamentalist tendencies and walks out, declaring *Lady Parts* "wrong". Saira blows up at the other band members for convincing her to participate in an interview that, in the very next episode, is shown to have made the band more popular and widely-known amongst their core audience. Her enraged meltdown drives her band-mates away. The season finale begins at this low point, with none of the band members speaking to each other because of how disastrous this successful marketing push turned out to be.

Ayesha is, of course, dumped by Zarina off-screen.

I am inclined to give the show a great degree of slack, considering just how ambitious it was relative to how little time Nida Manzoor was given to cover all these highly complex topics. At the same time, while I can pretend to not hear *Harry Potter* references in a British TV show, it's harder to tune out how the first season's biggest source of conflict is a duplicitous, devious queer woman who sells out her own community and sisters for financial gain, almost forces her girlfriend to come out without considering how it would impact her, and is shown literally "manufacturing racism" on-screen to better serve her own agenda.

After all, aren't we all tired of those privileged non-white queers who are more loyal to the West than to their own people? Who further the West's xenophobic narratives by talking about the homophobia and misogyny endemic to their cultures? The West is hardly free of ho-mophobia or misogyny, which is why uppity brown queers should keep their mouths shut about what "their own people" put them through, lest they make us look bad and single-handedly trigger the next US invasion of a foreign country. Jasbir Puar warned us about this! Don't these ungrateful degenerates know that talking openly about their oppression and asking for rights is basically doing the CIA's work for them?!

Don't they have any *izzat*?

It's really fun being a brown lesbian, thank you for asking. No matter where I am or whom I'm amongst, there's always a sin I can repent for. And to think I didn't even have to account for being trans.

This isn't really about Nida Manzoor's work. I still have more praise for it than criticism, which I hope is obvious. The Zarina storyline was just a very sobering reminder that even those who *get it* center the Western gaze so much that they end up coming down strongly on the side of "don't air out our dirty laundry", intentionally or otherwise. Even non-white feminists.

Because diaspora feminists have their own honor culture. Their own deeply-ingrained desire to present a simplified, sanitised version of their roots, to 'save face' before the Western observer. Patriarchy in the third world? Forced marriages? Honor killings?! Mind your tongue, imperialist, and get your own house in order before you cast aspersions on mine. I'll have you know that my people are actually far more gender-expansive than your piddly colonial binarist West could ever conceive of being! Have you ever heard of hijra?

And so even amongst our shield-sisters, we remain outsiders. We remain an inconvenient truth, an irritant to brush away lest our pesky voices rise too far above the din in a heated argument between Western feminists, both white and not. Talking about third world patriarchy is always doing the white man's work, the Western feminist says, to the white woman and third world woman alike. Remember that you are never free to speak such words with your two lips.

"Keep your peace," says the Western feminist to the third world woman, "and understand that this is about something more important than just you."

FOR YOUR TONGUE IS STILL YOUR OWN

The second and final season of *We Are Lady Parts* is, just like its first season, about a lot of things. It attempts to grapple with topics as wide-ranging as being 'visible' as a Black Muslim, whether influential queer people have an obligation to out themselves for the sake of 'visibility', and most emphatically the limitations on artists' speech imposed by entities who profit from their labor (subtle!). Season 2's fifth episode is a high watermark, a full-throated embrace of *WALP*'s more surrealist inspirations where Saira tries to write something more meaningful than a "funny Muslim song" and ends up suspended mid-air, choked by an invisible force, violently censored for even attempting to say the word "w#@!".

It is not a difficult message to intuit, or appreciate. Very often, the cost of visibility is authenticity, and marginalized people frequently have to consider whether it's worth it to cede control over the point and themes of their own work when the alternative is not being platformed at all. The tension regarding *WALP*'s clear desire to be about so much more than what it was given the time to be is palpable. The fact that it is subject to the limitations imposed on commercial art is vital to keep in mind when discussing it.

Even so, there are still critiques to be made. I am grateful for the existence of *WALP* as a joyous, rebellious, and decidedly flawed piece of media that centers the experiences of brown, second-generation immigrant Muslim women. That is what also leads to its biggest limitations as a feminist work, however. *WALP*'s feminism is non-white, yes, but remains stubbornly grounded in the experiences of the non-white *citizen*, of those who grow up alienated from their homelands and thus develop a complex relationship to their cultures of origin.

Unlike *Polite Society*, *WALP* is far more troubled about the *perception* of one's non-Western culture. Zarina's crime isn't simply being a queer woman who insists on talking about the flaws of her culture, but doing so where white and Western people can witness the conversation. "The personal is political", feminists have often said, and yet the anxieties amongst non-white Western feminists—of being deemed as from an "inferior", "savage", "barbaric" background—plague their approach to the unique double-bind women of color are placed in.

Manzoor's work here falls, rather uncomfortably, on the side of vilifying those of us who do not wish to sugarcoat our experiences. The West is not free of patriarchy and racism and unjust hierarchies, yes, and its ideologues are only too eager to claim its superiority to the lands it exploits and hollows out. Yet it remains true that lesbians and trans people and queer people of all stripes frequently emigrate from third world nations to the West. It remains true that many nations in the third world grant women fewer rights and less independence than is possible for many women to achieve in the West. We have a responsibility to consider why this is, and to resist those who ignore material conditions to advance a supremacist agenda.

But we cannot afford to be silent, deflective, or obscurantist about empirical truths.

PART THREE: "HAVE SOME SOLIDARITY"

I came across the tweet cited at the top of this essay when my friend from Iran (let's call her "Chem") posted a screenshot of it. Chem has family in the motherland and was understandably pretty worried about them in June of 2025, when both Israel and the US military began to grandstand about shows of force. We've talked to each other a lot about our respective cultures and the popular misconceptions that Westerners have about them.

One topic we've discussed extensively is the idea that in Iran, gay people are "forcibly transitioned" as a form of conversion therapy, to "trans the gay away". It is a popular talking point amongst British anti-trans activists, and a 2014 BBC article makes the claim rather uncritically. Chem has experience being trans in Iran and finds the credulity and motivated reasoning of Westerners rather distasteful. She knows of a case where a gay man was pressured into taking hormones as a cure for his sexuality, but the hormone in question was *testosterone*, not feminizing HRT.

As Iranian historian Afsaneh Najmabadi notes in her book *Professing Selves*, there is a wide gulf between something being *legal* and being *freely available*, or even destigmatised. Transition care has been legal in the West for decades, after all, while remaining thoroughly gatekept by medical professionals who rejected trans patients frequently. Najmabadi's interviews with officials, clerics, doctors, and activists on the ground paint a very similar picture of trans rights in Iran: legal in theory, heavily restricted in practice. Far from forcing anyone to transition, officials regard trans people with suspicion and often consider them to be deceptive gay people trying to transition so that they can legally marry their partners.

This makes sense if you view a non-Western society as a complex society in its own right, rife with its own movements, contradictions, conflicting interests, and oppressive regimes that marginalised populations must navigate. However, anti-trans activists do not care about nuance or fact; to them, Iran is a convenient case to cite in their crusade to present trans rights as at odds with gay liberation. Whether gay people are actually being forcibly transitioned in Iran is, to them, far less important than the utility of this fact about Iran, real or imagined, in manufacturing putatively 'progressive' opposition to trans people.

And as we can see in the tweet at the top, this reductive instrumentalisation of non-Western societies is hardly exclusive to right-wingers.

Chem has as little patience for diaspora feminist theatrics as I do. When she came across the cited tweet, she scoffed at the idea that White Western Feminists influence the foreign policy of imperial powers in any significant way. Are racist white feminists happy to assist neo-colonial efforts to manufacture consent for overseas military action? In many cases, they are. Does that mean that feminism or trans rights or gay marriage are, in and of themselves, movements that direct the flow of Western belligerence against hapless, insufficiently progressive third world countries? Hardly. The very notion is absurd.

As Chem said herself in a follow-up post: *"Being alive matters more than what you wear" yeah bestie literally tell that to the people killing Iranian women for what they wear while also failing to protect them from Israel."*

Chem's thread ended up catching the eye of someone I'll dub "Mags". Mags stopped by to inform us that they interpreted the tweet Chem was taking issue with "very differently". See, that tweet was directed towards those white, Western feminists who focus on what Middle Eastern women wear more than the Islamophobia and xenophobia directed at Middle Eastern cultures. "To me," Mags said, "that tweet isn't meant to speak to you."

Of course—why would Chem, an Iranian woman, make the silly mistake of thinking a tweet about the plight of Iranian women had anything to do with her?

Mags asked us to kindly find room in our hearts for solidarity with Western POCs, who were grappling with a racist society we had no experience with. As third world women, Chem and I ought to understand that when diaspora feminists speak, we're not actually part of the conversation. We are props for diaspora feminists to invoke in arguments with white women, not interested parties with concerns and opinions of our own.

There were actual statements from Iranian feminists on the topic of the Israel/US-Iran War, by the way. I'll transcribe a snippet from Iran's Feminist Liberation Group here:

"... 3. Don't forget the political prisoners.

As news cycles unfold, *many people are forgotten*. In Iran, countless political prisoners, including those on death row, are in grave danger every day. During the Iran-Iraq War, *thousands were executed in 1988 under the pretext of the conflict*. Let us not allow history to repeat itself.

4. Avoid idealising any form of state power.

Opposition to one oppressive regime does not imply support for another. All governments must be held accountable, whether it is Israel, the US, Iran or any other state. *Authentic anti-imperialism requires consistent questioning of all forms of oppression*.

5. *Focus on the voices of those directly affected*.

Empower those on the front lines—*not influencers who appropriate the narrative.* Find and support grassroots activists, independent journalists, and people who speak from their own experience.

6. *Iranian women and men are trapped between two forms of violence.*

Many people in Iran oppose the Islamic regime and at the same time fear foreign military intervention. They do not want to be used as pawns in geopolitical games. True solidarity means supporting their demands for freedom, without military involvement. ..."

Emphasis mine.

The irony here is that the specter of white feminism compels many feminists of color—frequently but not always diaspora—to center the white gaze in their analysis. Questions of patriarchy outside the Western context are treated not as relevant and vital concerns for feminists everywhere, but as racist Western propaganda, or a point of shame to talk around, downplay, and deprioritize. The third world woman is rendered either an agent of whiteness, who advocates for her own liberation at the cost of "shaming" her own people, or ignored entirely, reduced to a talking point in Western discourses.

She is, in short, treated by diaspora feminists the same way white feminists treat all feminists of color.

This was not the first time Chem and I had a conversation like this, nor will it be the last. Even as academics and feminists in the West purport to champion 'decolonialism', their attitude towards third world feminists, movements, and queer people remains tokenistic and extractive. The idea of Iranian women or Indian hijras or misunderstood, maligned third-world nations is convenient to the eternal game of rhetorical point-scoring between the people who *matter*—that is, Westerners. We should not confuse that with the concept of advocating for such groups, or even—perish the thought—listening to them in any capacity.

Non-Westerners are, ultimately, just a captive audience, here to applaud for our progressive Western saviors, or gasp as the unfathomable depths of the West's depravity are revealed. The racists say everything good came from the West, and the anti-racists say everything evil sprung from the original sin of the West's diseased conception.

The rest of us remember our place, and say nothing at all.

CONCLUSION: WE ARE A SOCIETY OF POLITE LADIES

"When you civilize a man, you only civilize an individual; but when you civilize a woman, you civilize an entire nation." — Patrice Lumumba, *Le Congo, terre d'avenir, est-il menacé?*

Let's talk about The Veil.

Regimes that ban the veil—or really any forms of cultural expression, especially those of religious or ethnic minorities—are always in the wrong. Such laws are nothing more than a way to criminalise being a visible member of certain communities and do nothing to advance the cause of a single multiply-marginalised woman anywhere. At best, they deny women autonomy, and at worst they create a no-win situation for those who were never given the option to choose, and have to risk incurring the wrath of either their own communities, or the state. These unjust laws are an example of how the women of marginalized communities are singled out for humiliation, and how their bodies are transformed into a battleground, a site for opposing patriarchal interests to vie for supremacy.

That said.

That said, refusing to be critical of non-Western cultural practices simply because they are non-Western cultural practices is the height of anti-intellectualism. Whether we're talking about white feminists who approach the topic with apprehension due to how much it has been poisoned by racists, or non-white feminists who would rather remain silent than risk their culture "looking bad", we see that people are happier to cede ground than stick their necks out for their espoused principles.

So I'm just going to say with my whole, out-of-lane, ex-Hindu chest: I think veiling is bad. I think that modesty culture is inherently rooted in treating women's bodies as sexual commodities, and that neither religion nor tradition are adequate justifications for misogynistic practices. It's that straightforward.

"What if it's their *choice*?" Then I can't do anything about it. Though that begs the question: how do you feel about the fact that under regimes the world over, women *cannot choose*? What if it's not their choice, and it's forced upon them anyway?

Are you willing to assert that that's wrong?

One might be tempted to repeat that timeless maxim: "Listen to the marginalized!" And indeed, if anyone is desperate enough to outsource all the risk of considering one's stances, making decisions and taking a stand to the nearest marginalized person whose skirt they wish to hide behind, they are welcome to do so. Do you want to find a marginalised woman who will tell you that the veil is not misogynistic in the slightest? Do you want to find a conservative marginalised woman? You will if you look for one.

Lila Abu-Lughod's essay, *Do Muslim Women Need Saving? Anthropological Reflections on Cultural Relativism and Its Others* considers this question at length. Can we find a middle ground between

Laura Bush pinkwashing the excesses of US militarism by casting impe-rialism as liberation, and the abdication inherent to 'cultural relativism' positioning all non-Western practices as beyond critique? What do we do when faced with Muslim women who say that they can be liberated without being 'Western' and taking off the veil, set against Muslim women who protest against the veil's imposition (as happened in Iran)?

It is true that the Eye of the West forever gazes upon us, eager to ex-ploit any possible division or instability to establish its own hegemony and hollow out yet another land, yet another people. At the same time, the West is also a convenient rhetorical tool for conservatives looking to cast any and all oppressive practices as an indispensable cultural artifact that needs protection from 'Western colonialism', even—perhaps espe-cially—when non-Western women and queer people are the ones speaking out against them.

Some of this is the result of liberation movements negotiation with their local contexts and asking questions such as whether an 'Islamic' or 'Hindu' feminism is possible. Najmabadi notes that the right to legally transition in Iran was, after all, secured through reasoning in the framework of Islamic Law. Appealing to the logic of the Nation—*any* Nation—will always be a fraught endeavour with limited returns, as Nations remain invested in patriarchy, natalism, and the management of internal hierarchies. Perhaps the non-Western feminist who decries the politicization of the veil by the West is very much against imperial-ism. Or perhaps she is trying to prove herself a modest woman who only wishes to secure her position and advocate for better treatment—rather than upend the entire patriarchal order destroying less-privileged women.

Enemy feminisms, after all, thrive outside the West too.

Further, the refusal to engage with empirical reality leaves exploitable gaps in progressive politics. Loudly refusing to acknowledge the flaws of non-Western cultures makes forming alliances across national borders much harder, and incurs the risk of alienating, if not outright radicalizing third world women, who see the misogyny they chafe against being summarily dismissed by the same people who champion queer liberation or anti-imperialism or trans rights. This incoherence in Western leftism stems largely from unexamined antifeminist sentiments as well as a mangled understanding of anti-racism that paradoxically ends up abandoning the most vulnerable non-Western populations.

Personally, I find I am tired of cowardice. Of apprehension. And I am, more than anything, tired of "feminists" who lack the conviction to stand by their own beliefs when it gets the slightest bit inconvenient to do so. I am tired of asking my friends to lend me their skirts anytime I wish to assert a basic feminist principle, and I am first and foremost tired of cultural and moral relativism and rank cowardice masquerading as 'progressive', 'decolonial' thought.

We can be a society of polite ladies, if you like. We can be meek and spineless and too terrified to think for ourselves, too terrified to speak with our own two lips on the off-chance that a racist or imperialist or conservative non-Westerner twists our words and appropriates our statements for their own goals. We can continue to watch the slow death of feminism in front of our very eyes, as any centering of women's rights or women's plights or women's pain is dismissed out of hand via any of a dozen academic, leftist-sounding rationales. Is that what you want?

Or do you want to be a *fucking feminist*?

Your tongue is still your own. So will you use it to stand with your sisters?

Which way, Western woman?

7

POLITICAL HETEROSEXUALITY, OR: THE TRAGEDY OF FEMINISM

FOREWORD: RENEE NICOLE GOOD WAS MURDERED AFTER I FINISHED THIS ESSAY

On the 7th of January, 2026, Renee Nicole Good was repeatedly shot by ICE agent Jonathan Ross. Good and her wife had been acting as legal observers in response to ICE activities in Minneapolis, and Good's extrajudicial killing at the hands of an unaccountable white supremacist force is hard to not see as retaliation for daring to place any limits on their rampage.

Good was called a "fucking bitch" after she was shot. ICE agents prevented medics from assisting her, and bystanders trying to reach her were told that ICE had their own medics to help—a lie. The reactionary media machine was quick to frame her death in terms that signalled Good was an acceptable target, an undesirable whose culling is to be celebrated and not mourned. Jesse Watters on Fox News mentioned that Good had "pronouns in her bio" and a "lesbian partner".

Fake mugshots and doctored images listing non-existent crimes circulated on X, and when they were easily revealed as shams, right-wing social media accounts resorted to the old, reliable tactic: pointing out that Good was a woman.

"I feel like I have been condescended to by a woman who looks exactly like this thousands of times", reads a widely-shared post on X attached to an image of Renee Nichole Good... smiling.

Just smiling.

Good's vilification by reactionary extremists in the wake of her death is telling. She was white and blond and a mother, but her queerness (and perceived proximity to transness, through "pronouns") was used to cast her as an enemy to the white Nation, to degender and mark her. At the same time the US President, in a statement justifying her execution, referred to her wife as her "friend", refusing to acknowledge the legitimacy of their partnership. In the days since, other protestors detained by ICE have spoken of being taunted by agents who called Good a "lesbian bitch" whom they "had" to kill—for her insolence, her defiance, her refusal to perform the role expected of white women under a rampantly Nationalist regime.

She hadn't known what was good for her, you see. She practically forced their hand.

Look what she made them do.

The following essay was written before these events transpired. It is not about Nationalism—not explicitly, though it does allude to the violence of Nation-building in parts. But it is an essay about lesbianism and lesbians and lesbian feminism, and the quiet, simmering hatred of those women who choose to love and be with women. A hatred that pervades politics both misogynist and feminist, both heterosexual and queer. It is an essay reflecting on the recent history of feminist movements and the quest for an ever-kinder, ever-gentler feminism that will, at long last, prove inoffensive and appealing enough to men's sensibilities. It is an essay about how, despite men demonstrating their investment in violent patriarchal politics, despite men proving time and again that they would rather tear up the social contract and uphold authoritarianism than countenance a world where women are free to exist independent of men, it is easier for us to hate and resent and abhor the women who point this out than the men themselves.

I present it to you with all the despair and grief and rage in my heart, and invite you to reflect on a world where men's feelings matter more than women's lives.

INTRODUCTION: HETERODOOMERISM

In 2019, Asa Seresin published the essay *On Heteropessimism*, boldly declaring in the subtitle: "Heterosexuality is nobody's personal problem". Echoing the longstanding lesbian feminist critiques of heterosexuality as an institution that structures our lives rather than a mere description of how one engages in interpersonal intimacy, Seresin nonetheless grounds his piece in discussions of the personal, specifically exploring how women relate to, view, and engage with (others', if not their own) heterosexuality. He begins with Maggie Nelson's admission in her meditation-memoir that "Heterosexuality always embarrasses me" and attempts to explore the implications of that confession, asking what it means for straight women to performatively disavow heterosexuality while nonetheless being fatalistically resigned to participating in it.

How can a heterosexual woman navigate love and lust when her partners are expected, primed even, to always disappoint her? To let her down in the myriad ways men let down the women in their lives, demonstrating constantly that they do not value women's internality or personhood?

Seresin's essay is provocative in a way that caught the imagination of a culture on the brink of patriarchal backlash to perceived feminist overreach. *Heteropessimism*, and the synonymously-treated term *hetero-fatalism*, became fresh buzzwords for social media denizens and pop-feminist writers alike to examine, dissect, and misinterpret in typical and expected ways. "I don't want to be, but I fear I'm heterofatalistic" reads an August 2025 article in an online wellness magazine, expressing a certain fatalism about being heterofatalist. A scant month prior to that, *The Trouble With Wanting Men* by Jean Garnett was published in an outlet no less transphobic and prestigious than the New York Times, chronicling one woman's exhausting attempt to remain optimistic about her dating prospects and explicitly citing the term.

It seems that despite their best efforts, straight women find themselves embittered, embattled, and embarrassed by the men who they wish to love and cherish, but who do not reciprocate these sentiments in meaningful ways.

That is not to say that heterofatalism is here to stay. Chanté Joseph found herself both explaining and defending her piece *Is Having a Boyfriend Embarrassing Now?*, which ran in British Vogue on October 25th, 2025. The response to her humorous observations on how women are increasingly coy and secretive on social media about the men they date was equal parts commiseration and defensiveness. One exasperated TikTok by Joseph, put out two days after the article's publication, even had her addressing the myriad accusations that her article was the product of her being single, jealous, bitter—a restatement of the ancient charge that feminism is the pursuit of the "unfucked", "frigid" woman who cannot find a good man. Joseph breathlessly explained that her article had many quotes from partnered women before being edited down and is not reflective of her own experiences, and that she is drawing from *lesbian feminism*, explicitly citing Adrienne Rich and Jane Ward in the comments. This is feminism from women definitionally incapable of being jealous of straight women, she almost screams, in a tone that I know all too well.

I almost feel bad for having to point out that being a lesbian doesn't actually stop straight women from accusing us of envy.

Seresin almost certainly never intended his essay to become a battleground over the utility of the words he dubbed to describe the phenomenon. Many straight women taking umbrage with 'heterofatalism', believing it to be a fad for immature single ladies or fed-up divorcees, would likely be surprised to learn that Seresin's piece is quite condemnatory. He believes that heterofatalism is little more than a soporific consumed by those resigned to never improving. He lays forth the charge:

"Spinning on its wheels, endlessly repeating, going nowhere—heteropessimists and queer theorists alike are convinced that this is heterosexuality's permanent fate. I think they're wrong, that there's evidence heterosexual culture is changing. But even if it weren't, we would have to believe it could, because tens of thousands of women are currently dying of it https://www.npr.org/sections/goatsandsoda/2018/11/30/671872574/u-n-report-50-000-women-a-year-are-killed-by-intimate-partners-family-members, murdered by their husbands, boyfriends, or exes."

Interestingly, Seresin seems to think that heterosexuality is a neglected field of study amongst its supposed detractors. Exhausted straight women and haughty queers all stand accused of wanting to leave heterosexuality behind without considering how this does nothing to help those ailed by it, those that Seresin insists cannot meaningfully abandon it. It is a call for feminism to confront the futility of a utopian abolitionism, a repudiation of the feminist history that once regarded heterosexuality as a moral failure. "Yes, universal queerness and the abolition of gender may be the horizon toward which we are eventually moving", he allows, in a tone I imagine to be cloyingly conciliatory towards us idealist militants, "but what happens in the meantime?"

What, indeed?

Chanté Joseph and Asa Seresin form a fascinating dyad in my mind —a cishet woman voicing her appreciation of lesbian feminism in defense of heteropessimistic attitudes, juxtaposed with the queer writer who coined the phrase to repudiate it as fundamentally poisonous, while obliquely denouncing lesbian feminism. The space between them tells a fascinating story that is, at its root, about feminist history itself: the doomed love between feminism and heterosexuality. The question here—the real, actual question at the core of all this frustration and disappointment and unrequited yearning—isn't really about how best to be a feminist or how best to approach the topic of heterosexuality and the way it structures all of our lives. The question is simply:

"Can heterosexuality be saved?"

It is a question that is being asked in the shadow of second-wave feminism and its advocacy of *political lesbianism*. Feminists in times past, even as they observed how heterosexuality is mandated by patriarchal regimes, once decried heterosexual women as traitors, as those who "sleep with the enemy". The idea that feminism and heterosexuality are fundamentally incompatible is one that has troubled feminists from before the heyday of lesbian feminism and continues to haunt us now. As we reckon with the antifeminist backlash giving way to the co-optation of feminism by conservative interests, culminating in the present-day escalation of conservative rhetoric that calls for a dismantling of women's rights in the West, the question lingers, and almost demands an answer.

There are two writers who could be described as queer whose responses to and discussion of *On Heteropessimism* highlight this underlying anxiety. The first, *Collective Turn-Off*, published by Sophie Lewis in 2019, approaches the question of heterofatalism as a byproduct of the increasing popularity of sex-negative feminisms. As someone who is familiar with Lewis through her strong family-abolitionist stance, I found *Collective Turn-Off* to be somewhat baffling in its condemnation of a cultural mood that she perceives to be regressive. Lewis contends that this is not a productive impulse, agreeing with Seresin that " ... the heterofatalist posture is still serving as yet another method by which white women like me can project outward our own cowardice and machismo – that is to say, our own aversion to vulnerability". I personally struggle to comprehend how expressing misgivings with heterosexual structures of intimacy—something Lewis knows invites punishment—is in any way avoiding vulnerability, or projecting machismo. The most revealing line in Lewis' piece, however, is the following:

"Indeed, misandry, as I see it, can never reliably be prevented from collapsing into transphobia."

... News to me.

The other piece under consideration, *Notes on "heteropessimism"*, is not a structured essay, but a series of bullet points from Shon Faye's Substack that was put out in December 2025, listing and building on her thoughts on "a term she can't escape". Faye is much more critical of Seresin, rightly pointing out that he muddles his own thesis by lumping together statements by queer women about a coercive system with complaints by straight women tired of being mistreated—and even statements by men expressing contempt for women!

"15. We do not need to call men's contempt for their own wives or hatred of women generally for not having sex with them 'heteropessimism'. *To do so obscures that it is simply better termed misogyny. 16. I* think grouping the way men express misogyny and the maladaptive, even mean-spirited ways women *attempt to cope with its pervasiveness* under one term is *ethically risky.*" [Emphasis mine.]

Faye, who has written at length about heterosexuality and dating men as a trans woman, unflinchingly talks about how many men "deeply hate the women they share their lives with and sleep next to", viewing their partners less as people and more as patriarchal status symbols. Her clear-eyed assessment of men's attitudes belies personal experience with these harsh lessons and an intimate understanding of the women who, having been repeatedly let down by the partners they chose, hoping against hope for the mythical "good man", are now finding themselves at their wits' end.

Faye is not entirely exculpatory of women's role in patriarchy—she's more than aware how the siren song of respectability and investment in the patriarchal positionality of the 'mother' appeals to cis women willing to barter for crumbs of status. She nonetheless asks us to recall that women who express a "hatred" of men are usually heavily policed for it, and reflects on her own complex feelings of anger, resentment, and distrust.

That said, Faye also cites Lewis towards the end of her piece, expressing her agreement with the anxiety that "misandrist inclinations" tend towards transmisogyny. "I think the current libidinal cruelty of TERFism is one of the main reasons why I won't allow myself to succumb to my own misandrist inclinations", she says, reasoning that her feelings towards men are something that she ultimately needs to make peace with.

My frustration with this conclusion is limited—this precise contradiction between being aware of how men treat women while being attracted to them is something many a straight woman has lamented. However, this pervasive fear amongst certain kinds of feminists—usually the queer and trans ones—that any strain of feminism critical of male-supremacy will always be doomed to reaction confounds me more than I can express. It speaks to a kind of feminist trauma, a reflexive recoiling that manifests when feminists are confronted with the inevitable, inescapable conclusion that our foremothers spelled out plainly. As if acknowledging how impossible men make it to love or believe in them will start us down a path that can only end with rabid transphobia and self-immolation.

I am familiar with these misgivings, and I understand where they come from. Queer people have been betrayed many a time by avowed feminists. Betty Friedan called lesbians in the women's movement a "lavender menace", and many of those radicals who protested and argued that they belonged turned around and expressed similar sentiments about trans womanhood. The sex wars were the apotheosis of this fear, this fury, this tension between recognising how sex under patriarchy is rigidly controlled and regulated for the benefit of men, and the libertine declarations of the burgeoning queer movement defending their right to live freely and engage in hedonistic pleasure. Seresin, Faye, Lewis, and others—we are all laboring under the burdens previous generations placed on us, still answering for their crimes and strug-

gling to live up to their expectations. So please do not think me ignorant or callous when I say that I can only muster the following response:

Boo fucking hoo.

PART ONE: YOU GIVE LOVE A BAD NAME

Since both Seresin and Lewis are emphatic about heteropessimism's popularity amongst white women, allow me to flash my race
card.

Loving Women: Being Lesbian in Unprivileged India is an ethno-
graphic account of Indian working-class lesbians by Maya Sharma,
published in 2006. The methodological challenges Sharma faced in
putting it together were significant—she was only able to find most of
her subjects through rumors and hearsay, looking into the local gossip
and asking after the "talked-about women". Over ten chapters, Sharma
meets with various individuals and couples, some under the thumbs of
their families, others who managed to eke out a solitary existence that is
frequently denied Indian women, all of whom faced significant challenges to be with the women they loved.

Marriage is the Sword of Damocles that hangs above the whole
text, prominently featuring in every story Sharma relates. Most of the
women she speaks to aren't able to avoid it, and some try to set boundaries with their husbands while continuing to see their paramours.
That is, in fact, how Sharma finds out about several of them—the
women's group she is a part of is approached by family members, both
in-laws and blood relatives, to try and mediate with or "talk sense into"
the recalcitrant girls.

One of the women Sharma speaks to, Rekha, is only allowed to meet with her under strict supervision. Rekha and her lover, Dolly, had attempted to flee together to Punjab, at which point their families filed a Missing Persons report to get the police involved. Upon being returned, Rekha was practically under house arrest and not allowed to meet Dolly.

Rekha's case fills Sharma with a profound sense of anger and powerlessness. She tries to slip Rekha her number during their meeting, so that she may be contacted in an emergency, but Rekha's uncle enters the room and snatches the slip of paper away. Sharma is ushered out soon after; her subsequent attempts to meet with Dolly are unfruitful, and leaves her with few avenues to assist either of them. The best she can do is to write a letter to the local officer asking him to help the two women. She never hears back.

A common theme in the lesbophobia these women face is a perception of sexual impropriety. Sharma's writing reveals that the lesbians she speaks to are rarely met with explicit homophobia, or a hatred that directly names their transgressions. Instead they are accused of "selling girls" or "prostitution", even when obviously in monogamous couplings. Rekha's uncle laughs at the notion that women can marry each other, dismissing the possibility out of hand—how can marriage occur when there is no man to take possession of a woman? Lesbianism, in being rendered an impossibility, is instead viewed as overreach, as women attempting to exercise sexual autonomy outside of their families' influence. In societies as patriarchal as India, this refusal to let patriarchs regulate your sexuality is the same sin irrespective of the actual reasons behind it, and invites third-sexing and vilification as a 'public', 'loose' woman.

This actually happened to one of Sharma's subjects, Mary, in her local women's rights group. Mary had joined after enduring decades of domestic abuse, but found that her 'friendship' with another woman in the group led to rumours and discomfort among their co-workers. They were called into meetings, accused of being prostitutes, and told to separate. In Mary's own words:

"What hurts is that *there is no space for women like us even in a group like ours.* It is here that we *dream of reforming society and changing the world* ... and it is in this very place that we face opposition. It saddens me because the years with this group, where we found each other, have been the happiest in her life, as well as mine, up till now. ..." [Emphasis mine.]

What struck me the most about Mary's case was this sadness, this sense of betrayal she's trying to put into words. Even amongst people who understand how unfair Indian society is to women, who try to help them through dowry disputes and widowhood and domestic violence, love between women is verboten, is something to be excised and punished and censured. It's resonant with the wider history of feminist struggle and its latent tension with lesbians. Betty Friedan kicked off the second wave by talking about the plight of wives and mothers, about menial domestic labor, the burdens of childcare, and the overwhelming pressure to not speak of the pain and violence husbands put women through. Her opposition to lesbians within the feminist movement stemmed from a belief that lesbian issues were irrelevant to the vast majority of women—and that lesbians were in fact a threat to feminism as a whole.

Lesbian feminism emerged in part to address this myopia. To argue that women outside of the private sphere are not free of patriarchy and are also victims of patriarchal violence, just a different kind. Analyses of heterosexuality as an institution sought to cultivate unity between lesbian and heterofeminism, to make women aware of how we are all compelled into relationships with men and how our societies make the same heterosexist demands of all women. Whether we accept or refuse the patriarchal bargain, we are punished, and a feminism that is truly for everyone has to recognize the common roots of our oppression.

That utopian desire for feminist unity never quite panned out, though. One can trace many narrative threads across the history of the second wave if one wishes, and the story of how lesbian and straight feminists never quite managed to see eye to eye is a prominent one. *Political lesbianism*, in particular, stands out as a battleground whose casualties and scars feminists still reckon with to this day. In its heyday, militant lesbian feminists held that it was in fact impossible to be a feminist while continuing to associate with men. They called for separatism, for rectifying extant patriarchal society by daring to imagine a radical, egalitarian future and living by its ideals in the present. In a 2016 Lesbian History Group event, Sheila Jeffreys herself recalled how this idea emerged from the leftism of the 60s and 70s—"living the revolution now".

The trouble with trying to build a new future while the existing order is invested in snuffing it out is perhaps obvious, at least in hindsight. Lesbian ethics and separatism is easy to see as a kind of early choice feminism, removed from its own materialist origins that were far more explicit about how little choice is afforded women. Attempts to overthrow heterosexuality through secessionism and trying to live as lesbian a life as possible certainly appealed to many women, but the point of patriarchy has always been that it's coercive. You can't escape it, dollface, and all that.

Frankly, many of the women who are most candid about heterosexuality aren't even feminists at all. Dworkin's *Right Wing Women* proved to have staying power in part because it shows how conservative women don't make excuses for men's violence, but rather resign themselves to it. They understand that they are women in a man's world, and so they try to make the best of a bad deal. Their rage at feminists and queer people—and indeed lesbians—appears to come from a kind of sunk cost, a reflexive lashing out at those who say things can be better when they already made their peace with how wanting better is futile—a juvenile fantasy we all must abandon, as conservative 'intellectual' Midge Decter put it.

Several of Maya Sharma's subjects, by no means trained feminists, voice similar sentiments about how inescapable patriarchy is, and how they struggle with the apparent inequality in relationships with men. It isn't just that they love women, but that love between women is free of the expectation of being lesser, of being subservient to a man.

After all, no one's as fatalist about heterosexuality as those who don't have a way out.

I don't actually like having to use the suffering of my people as a rhetorical sledgehammer. The pain and injustice my sisters experience weighs heavily on me, and even trying to write about it left me in profound distress for days. But the way whiteness is invoked in feminist discourses to imply that racialized and colonised and third-world women would never have cause to begrudge men or be critical of heterosexuality is frankly unacceptable. It belies how abstracted these conversations have become from the impact of misogyny on the majority of women worldwide, even as their names are invoked in pleas to be *nicer to men*.

I do confess that after years upon years of being treated with contempt for bluntly speaking about patriarchal violence, after being angrily denounced by women who haven't read any of my work but presume I must be condemning them for being attracted to men, and after subjecting myself to pages upon pages of the same cyclical debates on the topic of Why Feminists Shouldn't Be So Mean To Men even when the feminists under consideration were the exact kind of appeasers everyone keeps insisting we need more of... I kind of get it.

Of course some of the dykes wanted to fuck off to communes over having to put up with more of this unceasing bullshit.

Simply put, the endless relitigation of how we owe it to men not to speak plainly about their exploitation and abuse of us—a conversation that largely occurs between anglophonic women in certain socioeconomic spheres who have the ability to choose who to partner with to a degree that is mostly denied to women worldwide—*pisses me off*. If you are lucky enough to be able to determine what your relationship to men is, I would suggest you have a responsibility to do more than muse about whether it's unfair of you to say any harsh words about the guys happily mainstreaming incel ideology and birthrate panics into the modern political landscape.

Because that's the part we keep stubbornly ignoring in these discussions: that today, men everywhere want more patriarchy. A lot of feminists seem to be laboring under a collective amnesia of what the feminism that led us to this political moment was actually all about. We had nearly forty years of "patriarchy hurts men too" and sex positivity and making the case for anti-patriarchal politics to men. It did not result in the downfall of patriarchy, or a mass defection of men to the feminist cause. Instead, today we have Andrew Tate and fundamentalist Christian theocracy in mainstream US politics and Mark Zuckerberg going on podcasts to talk about how women in already male-dominated tech workplaces bring too much "female energy".

Since we all seem to need the reminder, let's revisit the feminist politics of appeasement. And if the feminism of white women is so objectionable, let's consider the very same history of tension between lesbian and heterofeminism within the Black feminist tradition.

PART TWO: FEMINISM IS FOR EVERYBODY (EXCEPT...)

LESBIANS

If there is such a thing as "third wave feminism", bell hooks is no doubt an exemplar of it. She began writing about feminism in 1981 when she published *Ain't I a Woman?*, which talked about the short-comings of the contemporary women's movement and put forth a feminist analysis incorporating race and class in addition to gender. Together with calling for the centering of marginal voices in feminism, hooks also maintained a commitment to accessibility and outreach. Of her most enduring works, *Feminism is For Everybody* is remembered as an accessible primer to feminist theory for all genders, written in 2000 to "rescue" feminism from its over-academic reputation. *The Will to Change*, written in 2004, is still widely cited as a feminist text that impassionedly and boldly makes the case for why men should oppose patriarchy too. She writes:

"The first act of violence that patriarchy demands of males is not violence toward women. Instead patriarchy demands of all males that they engage in acts of psychic self-mutilation, that they kill off the emotional parts of themselves. If an individual is not successful in emotionally crippling himself, he can count on patriarchal men to enact rituals of power that will assault his self-esteem."

The way hooks is recalled posthumously is somewhat at odds with how she was regarded while she was still alive, and indeed with her more radical feminist tendencies and influences in her earlier work. For all of her writings on the importance of "returning to love" between men and women, she always maintained that men are invested in patriarchy and have to commit to abandoning it. She also, in *Ain't I a Woman?* and her essay *Is Paris Burning?*, discussed how the emasculative excesses of white supremacy towards Black men results in a kind of overcorrection, an investment in hegemonic masculinity that is made to heal a "wounded manhood". I have seen as many men talk about hooks as just another man-hater as I have witnessed other men using quotes from *The Will to Change* to shut down feminist critiques of male-supremacy, which is itself a lesson in the utility of feminist appeasement. The radical critiques are forgotten, and the parts that can be appropriated are happily stripped from context.

In a sense, one could see hooks' work as a bridge between the second and third waves. It is one of the most notable attempts to correct the radical feminist movement's various issues with exclusion and militancy. In pursuit of that, she often writes of lesbian feminism as a misguided movement, and makes rather peculiar statements about lesbians overall.

The introduction to *Feminism is For Everybody* contains the following snippet about reformist feminists:

"... By accepting and indeed colluding with the subordination of working-class and poor women, they not only ally themselves with the existing patriarchy and its concomitant sexism, they give themselves the right to lead a double life, one where they are the equals of men in the workforce and at home when they want to be. *If they choose lesbianism they have the privilege of being equals with men in the workforce while using class power to create domestic lifestyles where they can choose to have little or no contact with men.*" [Emphasis mine.]

This is, generously, extremely weird. As hooks is talking about a specific kind of class politics amongst reformist feminists, it should perhaps be obvious that any 'privilege' they harness to "have little or no contact with men" is the consequence of their class, not their lesbianism. It is also somewhat bizarre to allege that being equal with men in the workforce is achievable for women, and especially for lesbians, given the prevalence of hiring discrimination based on sexuality.

Why mention lesbianism at all?

The introduction leads into an interesting claim that hooks makes, repeatedly, throughout the entire book. She expresses it most concisely in chapter 12, *Feminist Masculinity*:

"Conservative mass media constantly represented feminist women as man-haters. And when there was an *anti-male faction* or sentiment in the movement, *they highlighted it as a way of discrediting feminism*. Embedded in the portrayal of feminists as man-hating was the assumption that all feminists were lesbians. Appealing to homophobia, mass media intensified anti-feminist sentiment among men." [Emphasis mine.]

Taken together with statements about how feminism that was not "anti-male" was "suppressed" to make feminism look bad—made without substantiation—hooks is essentially charging lesbian feminism with being a tool of the conservative media apparatus. This is an interesting charge to make, given that as far back as 1971, right as the radical feminist movement was kicking off, it was Germaine Greer who appeared on the cover of *Life* magazine, billed as a "Saucy Feminist That Even Men Like". Greer—a career transmisogynist who in 2003 wrote a book about how beautiful prepubescent boys are and in 2018 derided MeToo as "whinging"—could hardly be described as 'anti-male' even then. Her 1970 book *The Female Eunuch* encouraged women to have more sex with men and be less monogamous—which has always been the kind of feminism elevated in the mainstream!

In chapter 16, *Lesbianism and Feminism*, hooks does her best to acknowledge and credit the contributions of lesbian feminists. The talks about having always been aware of lesbians and homosexuality growing up, and how when she began doing feminism, the movement was full of all sorts: "straight, bisexual and out gay women". She also mentions something interesting about the reception to her very first book:

"When my first book came out and I was attacked by individual black lesbian women, I was stunned. I was accused of being homophobic because there was no discussion of lesbianism in my book. That absence was not an indication of homophobia. I did not talk about sexuality in the book. I was not ready. I did not know enough. And had I known more I would have stated that so no one would have been able to label me homophobic."

We'll come back to that later.

This repeated insistence on how much she knows and appreciates lesbians is thrown into sharp relief when hooks begins talking about the history of political lesbianism and how upsetting it was for straight women to be told that they were man-centered. In addition to "being useful to conservatives" and "trying to be equal to men", lesbians must now contend with another allegation: that they made straight feminists feel bad.

With this context, I'd like to take a look at hooks' most stunning statement on radical and lesbian feminism, which she made in chapter 15, *A Feminist Sexual Politic*:

"Nothing challenged the grounds of feminist critique of heterosexual practice more than the revelation that feminist lesbians engaged in sexual sadomasochism, *a world of tops and bottoms, wherein positions of powerful and powerless were deemed acceptable.* Practically all radical feminist discussion of sexuality ceased when women within the movement began to fight over the issue of whether or not one could be a liberated woman, whether lesbian or heterosexual, and engage in the practice of sexual sadomasochism. Tied to this issue were differences of opinion about the meaning and significance of patriarchal pornography. Faced with issues powerful enough to divide and disrupt the movement, by the late '80s most radical feminist dialogues about sexuality were no longer public; they took place privately. *Talking about sexuality publicly had devastated the movement.*" [Emphasis mine.]

Firstly: the omission of "the trans question" in this summary of why radical feminism imploded is highly conspicuous. But leaving that aside for later, the idea that the feminist discourses on pornography and sadomasochism, a.k.a *the sex wars*, were the least publicized aspect of the radical feminist movement is breathtakingly ahistorical. Moreover, hooks here is implicitly agreeing with the premise that lesbians who engage in BDSM—then called 'sadomasochism'—do not have a leg to stand on when it comes to critiquing heterosexuality. This is not only a statement that is and was heavily contested by lesbian feminists, but it's one that the most transmisogynistic and sex-critical feminists, such as *Sheila Jeffreys and Janice Raymond,* subscribed to!

Taken together, hooks' discussion of lesbians and lesbian feminism in *Feminism is For Everybody* comes across as incredibly... petty. It is less a recounting of feminism's fraught history and more a listing of grievances, made by someone who seems to want to put lesbian feminists in their place for daring to critique heterosexuality and heterofeminists at all. Given all this, her insistence on how much lesbian feminists taught her about "pushing the boundaries of heterosexism" is somewhat trite. Especially considering what she writes as a thesis statement in the introduction to *The Will to Change* a scant four years after:

"It is a fiction of false feminism that we women can find our power in a world without men, in a world where we deny our connections to men. We claim our power fully only when we can speak the truth that we need men in our lives, that men are in our lives whether we want them to be or not, that we need men to challenge patriarchy, that we need men to change."

TRANSSEXUALS

Is Paris Burning?, a 1996 essay by bell hooks, is a critique of Jenny Livingston's 1990 documentary on New York city's ball culture, *Paris is Burning*. The documentary sheds light on this underground drag scene, where queer people who we may today recognize as fem gay men and transgender women of color compete in "balls", as a celebration of fashion, creativity and beauty amongst a heavily marginal population. *Paris is Burning* touches upon what life was like for ostracised queer people of color, organized into their own "houses" that are headed by a "mother", and is in a sense about finding joy amidst each other even as they face heavy stigma and violence. The resemblance to hijra houses and the guru-chela system is uncanny, and it shows how queer people across time and space have come together to form their own kinship structures in the face of expulsion and rejection by their so-called biological families.

In her critique of *Paris is Burning*, bell hooks asks: why doesn't this documentary about a marginalized and frequently ostracized demographic talk about their families more?

"Much of the individual testimony makes it appear that the characters are estranged from any community beyond themselves. Families, friends, etc., are not shown, which adds to the representation of these black gay men as cut off, living on the edge ... At no point in Livingston's film are the men asked to speak about their connections to a world of family and community beyond the drag ball. The cinematic narrative makes the ball the center of their lives. And yet who determines this? Is this the way the black men view their reality or is this the reality Livingston constructs?"

Many discussions of *Paris is Burning* consider how Livingston's positionality as a white lesbian must influence what she chooses to frame and focus on in a racialized subculture she is external to. And indeed, hooks remarks on how little space is given to the murder of Venus Xtravaganza, who died during filming. Livingston's motives and whether her work can be regarded as 'voyeurism' are and likely always will be hotly debated.

But I must ask: is the reason for the absence of traditional family, in favor of chosen family, in the lives of gay and transgender people of color during the height of the AIDS crisis not somewhat obvious?

And is it also not somewhat obvious why the film might make a deliberate choice to juxtapose "moments of pain and sadness", as hooks puts it, with the pageantry of the balls, where its subjects are celebrated rather than punished for their performance of gender?

Leaving that aside, the thrust of hooks' critique is twofold. She talks about how the femininity celebrated in *Paris is Burning* is, first and foremost, a "white, middle-class" femininity, and how far from being subversive, the queer subjects of the film reify and lionize the very same culture that oppresses them. This leads into her discussion of ritual, spectacle, and fantasy in the documentary, where she alleges that in making a spectacle of queer Black lives, mostly-white viewers will be left comforted by how aspirational whiteness is even to oppressed people.

"For in many ways the film was a graphic documentary portrait of the way in which colonized black people (in this case black gay brothers, some of whom were drag queens) worship at the throne of whiteness, even when such worship demands that we live in perpetual self-hate, steal, go hungry, and even die in its pursuit. The 'we' evoked here is all of us, black people/people of color, who are daily bombarded by a powerful colonizing whiteness that seduces us away from ourselves, that negates that there is beauty to be found in any form of blackness that is not imitation whiteness."

I confess that hooks' words here reminded me of a lot of scholarship written by cis academics on the hijra. Not only because of how she studiously avoids discussing transsexuality at any great length—save for an instance where Venus Xtravaganza is referred to as "him/her"—but also because of how she interrogates and dissects the subversive potential that these queer people of color apparently fail to embody. Is wanting to be celebrated akin to mainstream fashion icons—who in a white supremacist society will be disproportionately white—upholding white supremacy? Do queer men and trans women who "perform femininity" uphold the patriarchy?

These academic inquiries rarely hold any space for the reality that impoverished queer people are perhaps not trying to make a statement about the societies they are excluded from, but envisioning a reality where they may find acceptance and even recognition. Perhaps that is not as subversive as it could be, but do those on the absolute fringes, who are abandoned by state and family, bear a responsibility to only live life in a way that is subversive? Have they not paid enough for their subversion? Is ejection from normative life not sufficient evidence that they are not, in fact, upholding the norms that punish them?

When those who are expected to be masculine and uphold manhood find value outside of it, and dare to dream that we may one day not be reviled for our refusal, are we reinforcing the hegemony or undermining it?

Livingston may be external to the scene she chose to capture, and we may question the efficacy of her portrayal, but the fact remains that *Paris is Burning* put a spotlight on people that their society would prefer buried and forgotten. Many women like Venus Xtravaganza have died as she died without anyone knowing their names or wishing to remember their passing, and hooks' questions on the value of fantasy to such women, detached from the reality of why they do not dwell on their families, comes across poorly.

Of course, we're talking about an essay written in 1996. Even Judith Butler put their foot in their mouth regarding this topic back then, and in later years hooks must have given the subject more thought. In fact, in 2014, bell hooks sat down with Laverne Cox for a 90-minute discussion on race, gender and colonialism. There, hooks demonstrated her understanding of trans issues by—

"One of the issues I think many people have with trans women is the sense of a traditional femininity being called out and reveled in, a femininity that many feminist women feel like, 'Oh, we've been trying to get *away* from that.' Can you talk a little bit about that?"

By repeating the same charges of "gynemesis", "upholding patriarchy", and "reinforcing feminine stereotypes" that trans women have contended with since before *The Transsexual Empire* was written. When Cox talked about feeling empowered presenting as she does and asked whether her blonde wigs "feed into patriarchy", hooks commented "yes".

"bell was so shady," Cox would say in an interview with *Them*, after hooks' passing, "shady in a good way. bell would read, but there was always love there. There was always so much love, and bell had so much love for me ... It's complicated, and in some ways, she's absolutely right. And in other ways, *that gaze is subverted, because of the nature of who I am* [...] walking the streets of New York, early in my transition, throughout my transition it was about [having] armor, it was about survival. *You know, if I'm fem enough, and can get through, maybe I won't get killed today.*" [Emphasis mine.]

A relevant point here is how women of color as a whole feel the pressure to perform hyperfemininity at the risk of being degendered. Singling out Cox's heels as a synecdoche for trans womanhood's feminist failures is underbaked at best, and more accurately is a reflection on which parts of radical feminism hooks actually liked. The negotiation between how femininity is imposed on women, while simultaneously being degraded and held up as a marker of our inferiority, applies to trans women as well as cis women. Ignoring how trans women are discouraged from embodying a legible womanhood in order to make a point about how our feminine presentation is at odds with feminism simply reinforces that stigma and hobbles conversations about the conflicting expectations placed on all women.

Additionally, this rebuke of feminine-presenting trans women registers as somewhat hypocritical coming from someone who wrote so much about how it is wrong to shame women for choosing to partner with men!

It is richly ironic that one of hooks' most famous quotes could have formed the basis of an insightful transfeminist commentary: "The first act of violence that patriarchy demands of males is ... that they engage in acts of psychic self-mutilation ... If an individual is not successful in emotionally crippling himself, he can count on patriarchal men to enact rituals of power that will assault his self-esteem." These words demonstrate a remarkable cognizance of how men are expected to enforce sexed boundaries, and could have led to a discussion of the policing and violence that underlies transmisogyny. Men punish each other —and trans women—for being "like women", for failing to embody a misogynistic and extractive ideal of manhood.

Instead, reviewing how bell hooks regarded queer women in her work, how she condemned lesbian feminism and transfemininity by often holding queer women more accountable for patriarchal transgressions than the men who most benefited from misogyny and heterosexuality, it is hard to avoid the conclusion that she considered men more worthy of solidarity and outreach than queer women. It is a sentiment found repeatedly in feminist conversations, where the fear of male dismissal almost manifests as a kind of paranoia—how do we excise the specter of those man-hating dykes?

Trans women and lesbians are both a kind of feminist boogeywoman, posing questions of how feminism should regard those on the outside of the traditional, reproductive heterosexual coupling. And again and again, in response to revelations about the artificiality of sex differences or how men are incentivized to exploit women, we see a reification of heterosexuality. Whiteness is frequently upheld as a confounding factor in women's feminism, illustrating how an investment in white supremacy leads white women to adopt a self-serving feminist ethos, but investment in straightness is rarely given the same treatment despite it being perhaps even more predictive, across time and cultures. Every patriarchy asks its women to channel their dissatisfaction into reform rather than rebellion, into negotiating for better treatment over re-evaluating whether heterosexuality truly serves them. Every time the limitations of this heterosexual contract are revealed, even many feminists find themselves eager to shoot the messenger.

Just as hooks did when her Black lesbian feminist contemporaries criticized her first book.

PART THREE: FEMINISM IS(N'T) BOURGEOIS

BARBARA SMITH

Even if you haven't heard of Barbara Smith, you have heard of Barbara Smith. Co-founder of the Combahee River Collective and co-author of its famous statement, Smith can rightly be considered one of the godmothers of intersectional feminism. She also coined the term *identity politics* to stress how multiply-marginalized people—such as, for example, Black lesbians—cannot discount the effect their identities have on their marginalization or material circumstances. As a Black lesbian feminist who articulated harsh critiques of the women's movement of the 1960s and the exclusionary feminisms of some in the second wave, Barbara Smith is an under-regarded titan of feminist thought who, in many ways, was the first to say a lot of things that we continue to re-hash in circular discourses to this very day.

That *identity politics* and *intersectionality* are much maligned, misused, and contentious terms today, stripped of their origins in radical Black lesbian feminist thought, is no accident. There is an entire cadre of such women who were no less a part of the second wave than the academic and cultural feminists whose legacy has been allowed to usurp and define the modern conception of radical feminism. Smith arguably typifies a feminist ideal whose unburial from the annals of feminist history is fiercely resisted, and whose open-minded, class-conscious and unapologetic politics remains a standard to strive for.

Which makes her commentary on bell hooks' early work very interesting to revisit.

Black Feminism Divorced From Black Feminist Organizing, penned by Smith in 1983, is a critique of hooks' first book, *Ain't a I a Woman?*. Smith opens her article by frankly discussing how she had really wanted the book to be "good, incisive, and, most of all, useful", but instead it worried her "nearly to death".

"But from the very beginning I found myself questioning the conclusions she draws from the factual material she presents and being constantly surprised by her answers to the questions she poses. It soon became clear that despite its subject I was in profound disagreement with the assumptions of this book."

She starts with the book's first chapter, *Sexism and the Black Female Slave Experience*. Smith's and indeed hooks' statements on the topic have to be understood in the context of what Smith calls "the familiar argument that slavery and racism were worse for Black men than for women"—an argument that hooks says was usually espoused by "sexist historians and sociologists". Echoes of this line of thinking can be found today as well—in a 2016 Guardian article about "Say Her Name", Kimberlé Crenshaw herself spoke about struggling to overturn the misconception that Black women in the US experience less police violence than Black men do. Clearly incensed by the notion, hooks highlights the systemic sexual assault of enslaved women as well as the reproductive burden placed on them due to gestational capacity—or bluntly, "forced breeding". The overall point is one Smith agrees with, but she notes that hooks' argument relies on some bold and unsubstantiated statements (that have indeed proven to be ahistorical.) One of the excerpts Smith considers is:

"The sexism of colonial white male patriarchs spared black male slaves the humiliation of homosexual rape and other forms of sexual assault. While institutionalized sexism was a social system that protected black male sexuality, it [socially] legitimized sexual exploitation of black females." [The inline addition is Smith's.]

Bluntly: this is a very naive and yet definitive statement to make, and one that can be easily disproven. Even if the relevant historiography wasn't readily available at time of writing, it is not an assertion anyone should have been confident making. Smith dismisses it out of hand, pointing to lynchings as self-evidently sexual crimes against Black men, while also noting the way hooks dances around the topic of homosexuality and homophobia in order to make her point about sexism. This is a discomfort that, as we have seen, remains palpable in hooks' future writings as well. Already, Smith's apprehensions about the work are well substantiated—unlike hooks' argument.

"It isn't necessary to prove that slavery wasn't so bad for Black men in order to prove how very bad it was for Black women," Smith says. It is an observation that underscores hooks' rhetorical style as inflammatory and antagonistic to a perhaps detrimental degree, without regard for veracity and, as we have seen, focused entirely on advancing the strongest argument in the moment, even if it contradicts a later or previous one. Uncompromising feminist analysis has always been vital, but hooks is worryingly unconcerned about consistency or accuracy.

This tendency is one that Smith reveals in the book, over and over. For example, after downplaying the severity of Black men's suffering in order to make her point about Black women's abjection, hooks abruptly turns around and charges enslaved Black women with being insufficiently feminist. Smith zooms in on a snippet that is oddly similar to hooks' 1992 criticism of ball culture in *Is Paris Burning?*:

"By completely accepting the female role as defined by patriarchy, enslaved black women embraced and upheld an oppressive sexist social order and became (along with their white sisters) both accomplices in the crimes perpetrated against women and victims of these crimes."

Smith—one imagines tiredly—asks whether Black women wanted to be "equal" to white women by "accepting the female role", or whether they simply wanted relief from the state of being "sexual and economic chattel". Such allegations are reflective of a tendency in hooks' work (which persists in modern feminist discourse) that neglects the material conditions of abjectified populations and fails to consider the extremes of epistemic injustice wrought by existing at the margins of society. Must enslaved Black women, queens in ball culture, and impoverished hijras be accused of reproducing the conservative foundations of the societies that abhor and expel them? Is their desire to partake in the material privileges they are systemically denied itself conservatism, or are they allowed to simply want better for themselves?

This also draws attention to hooks' selective representation of Black feminist consciousness. *Ain't I a Woman?* holds (without evidence) that *if* surveyed, Black women in the 20th century would be shown to be more concerned with racism than sexism. Smith contradicts this by pointing to women like Ann Petry writing about male-supremacy in the 1940s, before digging into how and why hooks' discussion of both Black and white feminists is so erratic.

"Hooks' interpretation of events to suit her purposes is most blatant in her discussion of the women's movement. *She describes a movement I find barely recognizable. Hooks collapses the totality of feminism into its most conservative manifestations: bourgeois, reformist, profes-*

sional, and self-aggrandizing. It is the equating of the women's movement with its least progressive elements (long a tactic of the slick media and *certain varieties of anti-feminists*) which I think most distorts the impact of the book. Hooks describes the women's movement and white feminists in such derogatory terms that *it is hard to imagine why any black woman reading this would want any part of it or why any white woman would be inspired to change.* Yet ostensibly it is Hooks' purpose to encourage feminist opposition to sexual oppression in the black community and racial accountability among white women. It is necessary to examine how this fundamental contradiction in the book came about." [Emphasis mine.]

In her book *The Truth That Never Hurts: Writings on Race, Gender and Freedom*, this is Barbara Smith's definition of feminism: "Feminism is the political theory and practice to free all women: women of color, working-class women, poor women, physically challenged women, lesbians, old women, *as well as white economically privileged heterosexual women. Anything less than this is not feminism, but merely female self-aggrandizement.*" [Emphasis mine.] Smith is far from a stranger to the realities of movements plagued by unexamined conservative sentiment—being a lesbian of color will quickly teach you just how many people see you as lesser. Yet, she still writes about patriarchy and race from a place of intellectual honesty, rather than one of resentment. She does not treat liberation as a scarce resource and does not allow her personal experiences to be parlayed into a theoretical foundation that minimizes the misogyny less-oppressed women experience.

Her feminism is, in fact and deed, for everyone.

That is the understanding that Smith and I find so lacking in hooks' work. In her eagerness to make the case for Black women's place in the feminist movement and express her ire at their exclusion, hooks once again elevates the concerns of her own demographic by obfuscating the reality of how similarly all women are oppressed. Smith also notes that hooks speaks in a strict dichotomy of Black and white, going so far as to erase indigenous women and other women of color in declaring Black women as uniquely oppressed. A subset of the excerpts that Smith takes issue with are below:

"Prior to slavery, patriarchal law decreed white women were lowly inferior beings, the subordinate group in society. The subjugation of black people allowed them to vacate their despised position and assume the role of a superior. *Consequently, it can be easily argued that even though white men institutionalized slavery, white women were its most immediate beneficiaries.*"

"In America, the social status of black and white women has never been the same. In 19th and early 20th century America, *few if any similarities could be found between the life experiences of the two female groups....* In fact, white racial imperialism granted all white women, however victimized by sexist oppression they might be, the right to assume the role of oppressor in relationship to black women and black men." [Emphasis mine.]

Put simply, this is *a lot*. Smith is understandably baffled by how this sentiment "overlooks the reality of obligatory child-bearing, rape, and battering, to name only a few common female life experiences". Most egregious, however, is how lacking hooks' class-based analysis is. *Ain't I a Woman?* seems to only mention class to denounce the women's movement for accepting "the terms of white capitalist patriarchy", while the existence of impoverished white women—sex workers, farmworkers, factory workers—is elided to position white women as not simply untouched by, but *actively benefiting from patriarchy.*

"Yes, they had white skin privilege and were no doubt racist, but why doesn't Hooks examine the complexities of being white combined with being economically *and* sexually exploited instead of acting as if no such women exist?" Smith asks and answers her own question: "For one thing, integrating an analysis of class would not support her opinion that white women are not oppressed."

The degree to which this resembles the condemnations of feminism that Crenshaw observed amongst her students (in her 2010 paper on dominance feminism) is eerie. By ignoring the feminism and activism of her contemporaries, in forefronting the most reactionary elements of the women's movement while failing to even mention the socialist ones—that Smith actively participated in!—hooks lays the foundation for a feminism that defines itself in purely oppositional terms, that advocates for its own interests by denying the existence of others' oppression. If intersectional feminism is to be defined by the misappropriation of intersectionality theory that posits solidarity between white women and non-white women is impossible, and that white women and non-white women have no common interests, then bell hooks can be regarded as an intersectional feminist.

Which brings us to perhaps the book's most stunning declaration, whereupon hooks turns her ire towards the contemporary Black feminism she's revealed herself to be so unfamiliar with. Smith describes it as "absolutely heartstopping", before pointing to this passage:

"Some black women who were interested in women's liberation responded to the racism of white female participants by forming separate 'black feminist' groups. *This response was reactionary.* By creating segregated feminist groups, they both endorsed and perpetuated the very 'racism' they were supposedly attacking. They did not provide a critical evaluation of the women's movement and offer to all women a feminist ideology uncorrupted by racism or the opportunistic desires of individual groups. Instead, as colonized people have done for centuries, they accepted the terms imposed upon them by the dominant group (in this instance white women liberationists) *and structured their groups on a racist platform identical to that of the white-dominated groups they were reacting against.* White women were actively excluded from black groups. In fact, the distinguishing characteristic of the black 'feminist' group was its focus on issues relating specifically to black women. The emphasis on black women was made public in the writings of black participants. The Combahee River Collective published 'A Black Feminist Statement' to explain their group's focus." [Emphasis Smith's.]

After everything in the previous chapters, after studiously refusing to consider impoverished and queer and disabled white women, after saying that white women "benefited from slavery" more than white men did, as though the creation of a lower underclass in and of itself constitutes elevation, hooks actually *calls the Combahee River Collective racist*—against *white women*—for forming a group to advance Black women's interests in the very same women's movement whose exclusionary elements she supposedly condemns!

This is, to put it succinctly, nightmarishly incoherent. There is no defense of this—this is just hooks demonstrating a flagrant disregard for her own supposed principles for no reason other than, I imagine, a desire to declare her own work as superior to the Black feminists whose efforts she doesn't even acknowledge and who were actually fighting the battles that hooks purports to be so concerned with. After issuing this incomprehensible rebuke of Combahee, hooks in the very next paragraph calls for "bonding on the basis of shared understanding of woman's varied collective and individual plight in society" instead of this, as she puts it, "polarization."

What. The. *Fuck?*

There is something incredibly macabre about reading the co-founder of the Combahee River Collective and one of the foundational scholars of Black feminism have to address an accusation of anti-white racism, made in a book that is better enshrined in feminist collective memory than Barbara Smith's name. To read it knowing that *Ain't I a Woman?* was praised as a still-relevant work of radical political theory in a 2019 New York Times review. The work of Black lesbian feminists lies at the core of the concepts that modern feminists pledge fealty to without fully comprehending or engaging with them, but these contributions languish unheeded. Meanwhile, feminism that seethes with lesbophobic resentment and waxes poetic about how lost feminists are without men's input is lauded as our gold standard.

But white supremacist capitalist patriarchy loves to elevate "anti-male feminism", right?

Smith, I think, understood how this would go, even as she emphasized hooks' heterosexualism. *Ain't I a Woman?* pleads for interracial solidarity between white and Black feminists by explicitly dubbing antagonism between the two groups as "competing for male favor", "to be the chosen female group". The lesbian is rendered an impossibility, while hooks lambasts "attacking heterosexuality" as a dead-end for women who, she says, "[seek] to attain the kind of power they feel men have". Her bitterness at lesbian feminists once more manifests as bilious degendering, as spite towards women she seems to think can and do escape patriarchal punishment, making them women who aren't *really* feminists, like she is, but are just looking for an avenue to express "anger, jealousy, rage, and disappointment with men". Conversely, hooks espouses her own feminism as superior—gentler and kinder and more understanding of men, you see.

Unlike those man-hating dykes.

So begins the career of a writer, the same way it ended. Smith asks at the end of her critique: how, why, and for whom was *Ain't I a Woman?* published? South End Press was not, at the time, in the business of publishing feminist books by Black women. Why this book? Why this Black woman amidst a library of white male theorists? "The answers," she says, "are no doubt themselves lessons in the racism and anti-feminism that pervade white-male-left establishments." It is easy enough to give a platform to a Black feminist without checking how accurate her work is, if her thesis and conclusions are ultimately useful.

"But how better to disavow the significance of the women's movement than through the words of a Black woman who is supposed to be a feminist?"

I wonder if Barbara Smith knew how prophetic her words would prove to be.

Nobody else did.

CHERYL CLARKE

Cheryl Clarke is a poet and Black lesbian radical feminist. Her arguably best-known work is *Failure to Transform: Homophobia in the Black Community*, an essay that, just like much of lesbian feminism, seems more relevant today than ever. She begins with an account of her experience at the First National Plenary Conference on Self-Determination in New York city, assuming that a Black lesbian feminist like herself would surely be welcome within the Black Liberation Movement. Perusing the flyer that she says was "left on every seat", Clarke found the following passage:

"Revolutionary nationalists and genuine communists cannot uphold homosexuality in the leadership of the Black Liberation Movement nor uphold it as a correct practice. *Homosexuality is a genocidal practice....* Homosexuality *does not produce children....* Homosexuality does not *birth new warriors for liberation...* homosexuality cannot be upheld as correct or revolutionary practice. ... The practice of homosexuality is an *accelerating threat to our survival as a people and as a nation.*" [Emphasis mine.]

Oh, dear.

Written in 1983, Clarke's essay continues a trend of lesbian feminist insight that has been under-appreciated, if not largely forgotten, despite its clear identification of the patriarchal anxieties underlying reactionary politics. Clarke compares the text of this passage to the text of the 1981 Family Protection Act, which stipulated that federal funds could not be used to "promote homosexuality". Her appraisal of this resonance between the two bluntly outlines the fixation on machismo, manhood, and reproductive control that lies at the heart of all Nationalisms—even supposed revolutionary ones. This homophobia—this patriarchal agenda—is, according to Clarke, to the benefit of Black intellectuals who embrace "the Western institution of heterosexuality" and Christian fundamentalism to position emancipation as a masculinist, male endeavor.

One of Clarke's most damning examples comes from Amiri Baraka, who was elected Chairman of the revolutionary organisation Congress of African People in 1972. She cites a 1965 essay where he wrote:

"Most American white men are *trained to be fags....* That red flush, those *silk blue faggot eyes.* So *white women become men-things,* a *weird combination* sucking male juices to build a navel orange, which is themselves." [Emphasis mine.]

This fascinates me as someone who became familiar with the work of British anthropologist Morris Carstairs while I was writing *The Third Sex*. Carstairs' work on the hijra in 1957 is of a decided *Victorian* slant; he was cited in *Neither Man Nor Woman* declaring the hijra to be a form of "institutionalized homosexuality", betraying the "latent homosexuality" in the "Indian national character". The difference between Carstairs' words and Baraka's is one of race—not in the sense that homophobia is the exclusive purview of white, Western institutions, but that Carstairs' whiteness gave him access to a certain legitimacy and institutional backing that allowed him to declare an entire nation (incorrectly, sadly) as a nation of faggots while, at least for a time, remaining a part of the anthropological canon. It is harder to imagine Baraka's appraisal of faggy white men and masculine white women appearing in any serious scholarship.

Nevertheless, it does demonstrate how the act of Nation-building is fundamentally about boundary creation—our well-defined, structured, legitimate division of labor, set against the Outsiders' senseless, irrational, inscrutable ways that blur the lines. Perhaps Baraka was aware of the racist history of white academics citing the alleged gender-ambiguity of non-white races as proof of primitiveness and inferiority, and felt clever reversing the slander. Or perhaps he determined from first principles that one's manhood is always made most apparent by contrast with those deemed lacking. Either way, as Clarke pointed out, his Nationalism did not so much repudiate the Nationalism of his political opponents as it rhymed.

Compared to Barbara Smith's critique, Clarke's discussion of *Ain't I a Woman?* is much more brief. She, like Smith, isn't afraid to explicitly call hooks' work homophobic, calling attention to hooks' erasure of lesbian feminists and scoffing at her defense of heterosexuality. "Ain't lesbians women, too?" she asks; one imagines her winking at Monique Wittig. Perhaps hooks could have done with a little attacking of heterosexuality herself, reasons Clarke, given how much Black women chafe under its weight. Perhaps, just like Black men, the Black woman intellectual is

"... afraid to relinquish heterosexual privilege. So little else is guaranteed Black people."

Failure to Transform is, after all, a critique not of specific intellectuals and works, but of a wider issue in political movements that seem resistant to acknowledge the contributions of their most marginalized members. Clarke is as frustrated with the heterosexualism in Black revolutionary politics as she is by non-Black gays and lesbians who say that the Black community is uniquely or excessively homophobic. She details her own experiences of acceptance (with some exotification) amongst poor and working-class Black communities, postulating that a sense of empathy may be fostered between those cast out from white society.

In her words I see spelled out the same question that plagues her as it plagued Barbara Smith and Kimberlé Crenshaw and Nida Manzoor and all the women and feminists of color whose lives are made an endless series of loyalty tests. Who can I claim when I am racialized amongst women, a woman amongst the racialized, and a dyke amongst both? Who can I claim when no one seems to be willing to claim me?

Why do I keep on fighting for everyone when no one fights for me?

As a piece of feminist history, *Failure to Transform*, much like Barbara Smith's critique, reveals to me just how little has changed in decades. How lesbians of color were asking the same questions in 1983 that we ask today, and how difficult it is to keep fighting losing battles on every front we are drafted into.

I also get the impression that hooks never quite forgave Clarke for writing it.

Ain't I a Woman? was followed by hooks' next book, *From Margin to Center*, in 1984. It reads, in some ways, almost like an apology, with hooks echoing many radical and lesbian feminist points and giving her due to lesbian feminist contributions. She criticizes Betty Friedan's *The Feminine Mystique* for its narrow focus on middle-class wives, discusses the importance of ending compulsory heterosexuality, and even cites Barbara Smith—though, she takes care to reiterate that feminism "identifying men as the enemy" yields no positive results.

"Had feminist activists called attention to the relationship between ruling class men and the vast majority of men, who are socialized to perpetuate and maintain sexism and sexist oppression *even as they reap no life-affirming benefits*, these men might have been motivated to examine the impact of sexism in their lives." [Emphasis mine.]

Why do men beat, rape, and extract sexual and domestic labor from women? Because they are tricked into mistakenly believing that this benefits them, by the powerful men who actually oppress us all. How silly of working-class men to think that they gain anything from women being reduced to the status of personal indentured servant! (And hooks does, in fact, use the term "brainwashing", rather than considering that perhaps men are not merely morally corrupted into misogyny, but materially incentivized to uphold it.)

If only feminists didn't insist on demonizing men—telling men that patriarchy doesn't benefit them, and hurts them too, will surely make much more headway!

Amusingly, hooks makes a point of using Smith's own words in

Home Girls: A Black Feminist Anthology to continue grinding an axe with lesbian feminists: "Black feminism and Black lesbianism are not interchangeable. Feminism is a political movement and many lesbians are not feminists." That hooks' grudge against political lesbianism is as strong in her 2000 book as it was in 1984 is impressive, and hooks' acknowledgements of lesbian feminist contributions ring just as hollow in both. Though if hooks is sly in how she cites Smith, she's downright defensive when she addresses Clarke's essay directly.

"Clearly Clarke misunderstands and misinterprets my point. ... My point is that feminism will never appeal to a massbased group of women in our society who are heterosexual *if they think that they will be looked down upon or seen as doing something wrong.* My comment was not intended to reflect in any way on lesbians because they are not the only group of feminists who criticize and in some cases condemn all heterosexual practice." [Emphasis mine.]

Just as white feminists—whether "third wave", "decolonial", or whatever other subschool they subscribe to—demonstrate complexes about lesbian feminist critiques of heterosexuality, hooks too ascribes lesbian feminists like Clarke outsize power. While she nominally allows that feminists who critique heterosexuality are not necessarily all lesbians, she obfuscates that such feminists are still an absolute minority within feminism. Political lesbians cannot set the feminist agenda while they are outnumbered by political heterosexuals, whose commitment to toning down feminist critiques of male-supremacy has repeatedly won out. Whether or not the masses of women who are untrained in formal feminist doctrine are receptive to these ideas—and many non-feminist and even conservative straight women are quite cognizant and critical of men's power over them—the actual problem that hooks and feminists like her refuse to name is that these critiques make *them* uncomfortable.

Because there is no amount of genuflecting that lesbian feminists as a whole can ever do to make up for the transgressions of those few bullheaded enough to loudly proclaim the inherent feminist superiority of all lesbians. This fear—that attraction to and love of men simply makes a woman less feminist, less radical, and complicit somehow in her own oppression—is indeed one that women have wielded as a cudgel against each other since long before any dyke was allowed to voice her thoughts on the matter. It is an insecurity and a shame that is deeply embedded in the collective feminist psyche, and whether we use the term "man-centered" or "woman-centered" or "girl's girl" or "pick-me" or any iteration of the same core concept, it is a demon that we will never be able to exorcise for as long as we refuse to admit just how much this central tragedy of womanhood burns at our very souls.

Truthfully, straight feminists and straight non-feminists (and even queer men and the queer feminists still trying to apologize for Dworkin's existence) all desperately *want* there to be some magic fucking key that will unlock an arcane, secret reserve of empathy that men have, for all of recorded history, failed to access, squirreled away in their heart of hearts. We don't want to confront the inevitable conclusion, to endure the psychic agony that comes with finally comprehending one's destiny as designated resource for the ones with actual agency, most of whom simply find it more beneficial to dehumanize you than try to understand.

Imperialism is about borders and Others, but patriarchy is *intimate* in a way nothing else is. It freely invades our very homes, our bedrooms, our most private fantasies and even the bloody positions we like to do it in. "The personal is political" wasn't a paradigm shift, but the acknowledgement of a generational curse, an utterance of forbidden knowledge that has driven feminists mad since before we could name it.

You can't escape patriarchy, dollface.

And fucking hell we desperately, desperately need to.

CONCLUSION: ADRIENNE RICH WAS RIGHT

In the beginning, Adrienne Rich said that heterosexuality was an institution. Everyone promptly lost their minds.

Underneath all the fretting about heteropessimism, misandry, separatism, white feminists, and how much patriarchy hurts men, lies the actual specter haunting feminism: the lesbian. The figure whose crimes can never be forgiven, whose freedom from the curse of loving men inspires envy and resentment and fury in equal measure, who is too removed from heterosexuality to belong in feminism even as her distance from heterosexuality makes her a kind of feminist ideal that other women fear they will never achieve. She is too reactionary, too transphobic and man-hating and unfeminine and ugly, and also too pure, too fantastical, too idealistic, dreaming of a world beyond gender that is both too beautiful and too horrifying to allow ourselves to contemplate. Feminists recoil at the idea of being treated like her, desperately and loudly declaring that they're not all lesbians. Feminists wish they could be like her, when the weight of heterosexuality feels like too much to bear, when the yoke of the womanhood they're meant to enjoy and celebrate chafes their skin raw.

Dykes have been the sin-eaters and whipping girls of feminism long before the trannies made it fashionable, really. The Lavender Menace you can't quite rid yourself of.

Because feminists keep trying to rescue heterosexuality, and the obvious conclusion that it can't be saved breaks their little hearts. Abolish the family, abolish borders, abolish the state, abolish capitalism, and hell abolish *gender*, but abolish heterosexuality? Don't you know most women are heterosexual? Don't you know how much we love men? How could you be so heartless?

It really does feel like feminists are in an abusive relationship with men, sometimes. And just like those stuck in the endless cycle of betrayal and hope, they lash out at those of us on the outside of the dynamic, who have the clarity and therefore the temerity and the sheer obstinate gall to give them a frank prognosis. The endless whispered promises that "This time, it'll be different, baby" are more comforting.

And Wittig help us, but lesbians are collectively tired of being the bitch you all run to when you're in the mood to trash your ex right before getting back together with him.

I'd like to posit that hooks' empirically dubious statements in *Feminism is For Everybody* are less about what conservative media actually promoted and more about this persistent heterofeminist anxiety of being dismissed and lumped in with those cringey man-hating dykes who make us all look bad. It is an anxiety that ignores how much epistemic injustice feminism has always been and will always be subject to, how little awareness of any kind of feminism there is in the mainstream, and how even the mildest feminist critique can and will be summarily dismissed by antifeminists because antifeminists are not beholden to what is true. The dismissal of feminism as too loud, too radical, and too misandrist happened during suffrage just as it happened during the second wave and the third wave and still happens today, despite how thoroughly lesbian feminists of all stripes have been relegated to the dustbin of history.

So let me conduct an autopsy on the grand, decades-long, misguided heterofeminist experiment instead of further jabbing at everyone's guilty consciences about how they treat those angry, ugly, unfeminine, man-hating dykes. It's over, girl. You gave him everything he wanted, and his response was to demand even more, to find religion and talk about how nice it would be to have a tradwife who can't vote or divorce him. Feminism cannot make straight men any promises that are more appealing than the depths of domination and depravity patriarchy has on offer, and the protracted, tortured, overdue reckoning with the fact that men demonstrate sex-class solidarity and will protect their collective sex-class interests—even if it means giving more powerful men more power over them—is what's making women everywhere have a crisis of faith in feminism.

I do not mean that all women absolutely must shave our heads and march to the nearest bra crematorium en masse. Lysistrata is not quite a feasible tactic in a world where men's most valued freedom is their ability to coerce sex with impunity. At the same time, consider which developments the modern men's grievance movement has organized in response to. Birthrates are falling because today, women everywhere are more educated, more autonomous, more independent, and more able to establish lives and incomes and stability outside of male-dependence. Women who opt to co-parent with other women instead of remarrying, or can avail of abortions, or be childless or gay or transgender or sluts with access to contraception at unprecedented rates may not constitute a literal worldwide sex strike, but our increased ability and demonstrated desire to opt out of the heterosexual contract is frankly being treated just like one.

So I apologize, personally and deeply and from the bottom of my heart, for every lesbian who has ever shamed women for loving or sleeping with men. I say that because more than ever, we need to forgive each other for the sins of feminists past, present, and future, and confront the reality that even when disenfranchised men have the will to change, they will frequently and with frightening consistency choose to make things worse for us. I say that knowing that it probably won't do much good, because whether or not there are actual political lesbians and separatists going around shaming women, it's the political lesbian in all our minds whose words cut deepest.

Personally, I think we need women to stop caring about whether wanting to fuck men makes them traitors to the sisterhood, and more importantly we need to them to stop pre-emptively crashing out at each other over such fears. What good has it done? What good will it possibly do?

In a similar vein, we need to stop betting on a horse that has, repeatedly and consistently, kicked us in the head every time we've done so. Feminism cannot afford to wait for those demanding no-fault divorce and a government-assigned girlfriend to come around.

What we need most of all, though, is to recognize that feminist struggle has to build power and structures outside of the family, outside of the state, and outside of heterosexuality. We need to be ready to hold each other as the endless war that is simply living as a woman continues to take a toll on each and every one of us, and we need to remain dauntless in the face of a resurgent, uncaring, and gleefully cruel libidinal political moment that wants nothing less than to reduce us to the state we've fought so long to escape.

How do we fix heterosexuality? I don't really know or care. I want women to be safe. I want them to be able to own property and earn incomes and be equally able to pursue single motherhood and single spinsterhood. I want women to be free—free of gendered obligations, free to escape prisons of financial dependence and social ostracism for the crime of refusing to be male property. The question of love and the crisis of masculinity in response to expectations of egalitarianism in intimacy is, to me, a secondary concern that will remain so for at least decades. Can we liberate women first, before we start pontificating about how best to liberate sex?

The defanging of feminist activism actively threatens our ability to meaningfully respond to misogyny as an animating political force. And at every turn, there are women whose investment in patriarchy and readiness to call compromise and complicity "feminism" will undermine the project of liberation. But the existence of collaborators doesn't mean patriarchy has no gender, or that there isn't a clear gender hierarchy that the most reactionary elements of modern politics want to enforce. That women can betray feminism doesn't mean feminism must abandon the woman, especially when she needs feminism the most.

So, knowing all the risks, keeping in mind all of the fraught history and the way it can and has gone wrong, I implore: stop running from the specter of the lesbian. Consider that no struggle can be won by asking at every turn if the terms of resistance are acceptable to those most opposed to liberation. And if the idea of not putting a love for men at the center of feminism disquiets you so, consider this question that I know makes me an asshole to say out loud, but that I have to ask all the same:

Are you going to wait forever for men to love you back?

8
UNDERSTANDING TRANSMISOGYNY, PART SIX: EPISTEMIC VANDALISM

"I am a monument to all of your sins."

— The Gravemind, *Halo 2*

Trigger Warning: the incalculable violence that has for aeons chewed up and spat out our sisters and our foremothers and that will continue to consume the lives and dignities of women whose names we'll never know until the day we finally bring about its end.

INTRODUCTION: "GENDER AFFIRMATION"

In 2025, researchers from the Universitat Oberta de Catalunya published a study in the journal Revista de Derecho Penal y Crimi-nología, called *Mujeres Cis y Transexuales que Practican Sexo de Pago:*

Involucracion y Consecuencias (or: *Cisgender and Transgender Women Who Engage in Paid Sex: Involvement and Consequences*). The researchers had interviewed 76 sex workers—largely migrants, 50 of them cis, 26 transsexual—and according to the article, sought to challenge prevailing orthodoxies and narratives surrounding sex work and trafficking.

It was a short and edifying read, concluding with a plea for decriminalization (or at least, fewer regulations that make the lives of sex workers harder) and cautioning against a certain tendency to believe all sex workers are trafficked. The study indicated that about 25% of the surveyed participants were "deceived by another person"—so could be considered 'trafficked'—while 84% indicated they made the decision "due to a lack of financial resources".

One section of the article in particular stood out to me, though: the section on transsexual women. An interesting assertion about their motivations caught my eye:

"However, in the case of transsexual women, the decision is often related to a desire to affirm their sexual identity and to a sense of fun."

For those less familiar with the discursive currents of online Gender-Conservative communities, this phrase in particular registered as alarming because of the pervasive transmisogynistic talking point that sexual violence against trans women is "less severe" than that against "real women" because—and I have heard this verbatim—we asked for it. The "choice" to be transsexual, to pursue transition and present to the world as a woman is cast entirely as a sexual fetish and an open invitation to be violated. The transmisogynist is almost convinced that trans women *cannot* be assaulted because we view any assault or sexual exploitation as *affirming*—and presumably because the Amazon basics skirt is too short, too.

So to ascribe the principal motivation of transsexual sex workers to "a sense of fun", when the article's *very next paragraph* admits that 61% of the transsexual women interviewed began sex work *as children*, felt more than a little dissonant.

Since I don't speak Spanish, I had to rely on machine-translation in order to investigate the actual text of the paper, so it's possible that there is some nuance that escaped me. At the same time, the English-language article seemed to have drawn this conclusion from the paper itself, though it is difficult to understand how the researchers could have concluded what they did based on the actual excerpts of these women's testimony. The study claims that one of its main contributions is the comparison between cis and trans women, and that "it is worth highlighting that [trans women] engage in paid sex *not so much as a result of pressure from third parties* but rather as an option to serve personal goals, among which the *need to affirm their sexual identity* stands out." [Emphasis mine.]

Meanwhile, here are some of the testimonial snippets from trans women the researchers provided.

"My status as a transgender woman forces me to work in prostitution. If I don't have an employment contract, how else do I make a living?" (ID40)

"My transgender status: I'm a trans woman, and prostitution is your survival option. Who hires a trans woman?" (ID47)

"Because I wanted money and didn't have job opportunities, and I also wanted my female body." (ID76)

These statements certainly point to external, economic factors that the women clearly identified, pointing to their lack of options, not "lack of pressure". It seems that the desire for transition that one of them expressed, *alongside employment discrimination*, was what the cis researchers chose to zoom in and focus on.

There is also a longer statement from one of the trans participants, whose translation I've reproduced here:

"I wanted money, parties, drugs, surgery, and everything that made me more feminine. When I arrived in Spain, I wanted to find a new life, where I could be a woman and start from scratch, but once here, I continued with the same old thing. Besides, I didn't have any papers, **so what else could I do** ...? I wanted to feel like a complete woman. I wanted surgery, **my family didn't understand the situation; it was a very closed-minded town, and they were embarrassed**. I started experimenting, and trying to raise money for the surgery. I had breast surgery **at age 15**." [Emphasis mine].

Not only do the researchers rather selectively overlook the socioeconomic factors that compel these women to take up sex work, they further conclude that trans women have "a more recreational tendency that leads them to experiment with and relativize the negative impact of the activity". Such an inference is almost certainly derived from the researchers refusing to view access to transition care as a *necessity*, and considering trans women resorting to sex work as seeking to fund a frivolity. There is no engagement with *their own finding* that most of the trans women faced disownment and societal transmisogyny that led them to start as minors, and that perhaps their attraction to the "glamorous lifestyle" they were promised could be treated as more in line with the other deceived (cis) women than as "a recreational tendency".

A fundamental incuriosity and frank indifference towards the reality of trans women's oppression pervades these remarks, which despite finding that trans women enter the trade younger, stay longer, and have a harder time leaving than cis women, never once cares to connect that to wider transmisogynistic structures and forces. Instead, cis people's biases, their insistence on viewing us as fetishists first and marginalized women never, takes precedence and is featured over and above their own data, their own findings, and indeed, over and above *trans women's own fucking words.*

This unnamed, unexamined cissexism is hardly limited to this one study, this one topic, or even this one discipline. Regular readers may recall a section of *The Third Sex*, where Serena Nanda relates a hijra's account of being deemed a not-woman by a third party due to her inability to give birth, and claims that as evidence that hijra *view themselves as not-women.* This despite the fact that in the story itself, the hijra subject asserts, rather unambiguously, "*I am a lady.*"

In fact, this blatant scholarly gaslighting, this impetus to demand readers ignore the evidence of our own lying eyes, manifests even in Janice Raymond's *Transsexual Empire.* In the third chapter of that book (*Mother's Feminized Phallus, Father's Castrated Femme*), she discusses interviewing 15 transsexuals and finding them all to believe and reinforce "feminine stereotypes". She also includes this little tidbit.

"R. also made the very important point that one of the reasons transsexuals may seem to conform exaggeratedly to the stereotype is that *they have to prove to the gender identity clinics that they can pass (i.e., live, work, dress, and be accepted) as women.*" [Emphasis mine.]

Despite being *told the fucking answer*, Raymond had no interest in examining the hypersurveillance and policing employed by male-led institutions gatekeeping critical healthcare from vulnerable women, and instead proceeded with her agenda of vilification.

We are not seen as thinking, feeling, hurting women, but as curiosities and symbols and exoticities, as freaks to be discussed and consumed and fucked, but never consulted, never respected, and never honestly seen as equal.

And all of cis society, especially its fucking "intellectual arm", its *vaunted episteme*, stands guilty of this shameless, unrepentant, libidinous dehumanization.

PART ONE: AUTOSAPIOPHILES

MAD TRANNY DISEASE

The history of trans women's pathologization is severely under-discussed, even amongst proponents of trans rights, who often default to leaving the availability, legality, and allowance of transition "up to the experts". Many a well-meaning advocate has uttered some variant of "the science is on our side", unwittingly eliding how "the science" has for a very long time treated queerness as an aberration to correct, or an ailment to be cured. Modern trans history is, in many ways, inseparable from the history of its vilification, regulation, and attempted eradication by medical establishments.

The earliest theories that attempted to grapple with the existence of the transsexual woman conceptualized us as a sort of tragic homosexual gone mad, a faggot so desperate to be "fucked by real men" that she begins to desperately desire womanhood. German psychiatrist Richard von Krafft Ebing published *Psychopathis Sexualis* in 1886 as a treatise on "sexual deviance"; his belief was that homosexuality is a "condition" that manifests primarily in (cis) men who wish to have sex with (cis) men "as women do". (Readers may recall that this reflects wider patriarchal discourses on penetrability that could, under some social regimes, spare those who take the 'active', *penetrating* role in sex from the stigma of being branded homosexual.)

Berlin's Third Sex, published in 1904 by Magnus Hirschfeld, himself a gay man, took a rather more sympathetic and even celebratory view of Wilhelmine Germany's gay subcultures. (This is the same Magnus Hirschfeld whose Institute for Sexual Research was targeted by the Nazis, to burn its books and research papers.) He detailed stories of transvestism, cabaret, and gender-variant individuals, and his choice of title illustrates how the concept of an 'in-between' or third sex in scholarship has always been oriented around the *penetrable male* —'men' who 'take it'.

Of course, the destruction of Hirschfeld's Institute and the Nazi regime's retrenchment of the homophobia he fought against all his life had implications for the academic perception of transsexuality. US psychiatrist David Cauldwell launched the next volley in the century-long war between scholars of sex and queer communities, coining the term 'transsexual' in his 1949 essay with the clever, *clever* title of *Psychopathia Transexualis*. Trans women are pathologized as having "criminal and unsocial tendencies", and Cauldwell's prescription for our gender-madness is to just... not. Could us icky trannies just stop trying to crossdress and change sex? The essay holds that transsexuals do not need gender-affirming care and instead need to be freed from this aberrant, unnatural compulsion—that is, it advocates for conversion therapy, for discouraging transsexuals from exhibiting 'gender-variant' behavior, and treating transsexuality as a disease to cure.

It was this prevailing consensus that endocrinologist and sexologist Harry Benjamin was responding to when he began to advocate for providing (some) transsexuals with access to transition care. Benjamin, in fact, worked with Cauldwell and other psychiatrists, with whom he disagreed on the question of providing trans patients with surgical and hormonal treatments. He codified his approach in *The Transsexual Phenomenon*, published in 1966, where he would discuss his diagnostic criteria for those he calls the "true transsexuals".

Benjamin had a "Sexual Orientation Scale" ranging from 1-6, with "transvestites" at 1 and "true transsexuals" at 6. Number 6 is our familiar faggot-gone-mad, she who only yearns for a Real Man and is simply too distressed by her lack of vagina and womanly attributes to be a productive, functional member of society. It is the sixers (and perhaps the occasional fiver) who Benjamin designates as a worthy, deserving recipient of the magnanimous gifts of sex reassignment surgery and oestrogen. The rest—those of us who aren't distressed enough about our sex organs, or who for some arcane and incomprehensible reason aren't irresistibly drawn to men—were welcome to, scientifically speaking, go fuck ourselves.

Though Harry Benjamin credits the high-profile Christine Jorgensen with 'furthering his understanding' of trans issues, he largely did his work and spoke out without the input of trans women (aside from white, middle-class, conservative 'transgenderist' Virginia Prince). While his model may have been an improvement over the categorization of transsexuality as a criminal disorder, it encoded certain cissexist biases regarding the perception of trans women into its recommendations. Specifically, it sought to rank trans women by how "deserving" we are of treatment, based on how well we conform to an ideal of womanhood centered around heterosexuality—that is, male-supremacy and male-attraction. By contrast, those of us who fell short of this ideal were still stigmatized, still considered "fetishists" or cross-dressers, regarded as no more than men who got a sexual thrill by behaving like or thinking of themselves as women. The Benjamin scale established a still-antagonistic psychiatric approach, of discernment between the mad faggots genuinely in distress and the male perverts in lingerie who aren't *really* transsexual but still seek transsexual care for... reasons. Gross ones, probably.

Benjamin's ideas were influential enough that WPATH—the organization of (largely cis) medical professionals that sets the current Standards of Care for trans people worldwide—was initially named HBIGDA, or the Harry Benjamin International Gender Dysphoria Association. The most up-to-date versions of WPATH's SoC purport to be much more enlightened and current and oh so much more respectful of trans people's delicate little sensibilities, but as any good lawyer knows, there is a wide gulf between pretty words and actual implementation. Many Gender Identity Clinics worldwide do not follow an informed consent model for access to healthcare, and a great many seem to be using SoC a few versions out of date—erroneously, one hopes. While the meaningless drivel that trannies spout is of no great import, I will admit that an awful lot of trans women I've spoken to report horror stories when recounting their interactions with psychiatrists and clinicians and endocrinologists, who treat every evaluation as an investigation, trying to sniff out the tell-tale signs that their patients are insufficiently feminine or not actually raging mancock addicts. Many of us have been asked deeply invasive questions about how we masturbate and what our sexual fantasies are like—even as minors seeking care.

If any cis readers sat up in their seats and wondered, "Wait, isn't that illegal, or at least grossly inappropriate?", then congratulations! You're starting to get how little anyone gives a fuck about trannies.

This does not even touch upon RLE, or "real-life experience", an outdated (yet still not entirely abolished!) practice of forcing trans people to live full-time as their 'chosen' genders, for multiple years, but without any transition care. Readers who may be aware of the phenomena known as 'patriarchy', 'homophobia', and even the esoteric concept of 'transmisogyny', perhaps realize how this amounts to little more than hazing, torture, and a challenge to survive as a visibly gender-variant, 'deviant' individual—irrespective of how hostile one's material circumstances may be or how one's very *employers* may react—for the potential reward of getting to transition bodily afterwards.

Simply put, many medical "experts" on trans people and transition care do not appear to have our best interests at heart. By acting as gatekeepers to lifesaving medication, predicated on navigating byzantine psychosexual gauntlets and not pissing off your asshole doctor too hard, these 'professionals' not only wield an undue amount of power over trans patients, not only are enabled to neglect, under-dose, and dismiss large numbers of people in need, but also are in a position to browbeat and abuse vulnerable, marginal, precarious people. Which occurs not infrequently. The very foundation of knowledge about trans people is this hostile, antagonistic, and cissexist milieu that still in many ways pathologizes and villanizes us, and many medical institutions entrusted with the responsibility of transition care are not merely hilariously unaccountable to our wellbeing, but largely structured to treat our existence as a problem to manage, guinea pigs to dissect, and indeed a plague to keep under control.

In fact, the modern anti-trans movement relies heavily on this history, building on the academic and scholarly disgust with trannies to inform contemporary propaganda and conjure the demonized specters of perverted, predatory males trying to access "women's spaces" for sexually deviant and rapacious reasons. Benjamin did not invent the 'fetishistic transvestite'—Hitchcock's *Psycho* was released in 1960, after all—but it did give legitimacy to an already culturally-prevalent idea.

Unattracted to men, aroused by women's clothing, patriarchal ideas of gender constructed this she-male, this monster encroaching upon bathrooms and prisons and sports to snatch up your poor, innocent girls.

Boo.

This gendered boogeywoman has many architects, but none so notorious as the Canadian fossil who is aroused by the idea that he has any idea worth speaking aloud. For 'transvestite' isn't quite what trans women as a whole and trans lesbians in particular are slurred as these days—there's a much more colorful term that our biggest fans are overly fond of.

Autogynephile. The monstrous creep who commits the cardinal sin of looking at her immaculate fit in the mirror and thinking, "Hot stuff".

There's a Margaret Atwood quote I always think of when discussing this subject: "Male fantasies, male fantasies, is everything run by male fantasies? Up on a pedestal or down on your knees, it's all a male fantasy: that you're strong enough to take what they dish out, or else too weak to do anything about it. *Even pretending you aren't catering to male fantasies is a male fantasy*: pretending you're unseen, pretending you have a life of your own, that you can wash your feet and comb your hair unconscious of the ever-present watcher peering through the keyhole, peering through the keyhole in your own head, if nowhere else. *You are a woman with a man inside watching a woman.* You are your own voyeur." [Emphasis mine.]

One might argue that in a society whose foundation is patriarchy, where those sexed as men are empowered to regard those sexed as lesser as though they are consumable sexual commodities, many of us excluded from the humanity afforded manhood learn that our self-worth is rooted almost entirely in our desirability. That feeling a sense of comfort, power, safety, and yes, even a certain erotic fulfillment, in the idea of oneself as a desirable object who may lack patriarchal agency but can nonetheless inspire devotion and fixation and covetousness with a mere flash of the ankle, is simply what "women's sexuality" is conditioned to be. That perhaps, far from observing some inconceivable paraphilia, sexologists simply observed "women's sexuality" in "male subjects", and freaked the fuck out as their pretty little heads couldn't cope with the ramifications that has for a society founded on the sex-class differ-ence.

Alternatively, one might become a figurehead for an international hate movement because they were the only ones who saw any merit to the shit-doodles you farted out on some loose leaf in the 80s.

I CAN NEVER REPAY CHRISTA PETERSON

Christa Peterson is a Philosophy PhD student who, in 2023, left critical comments on a few 'research' papers on PubPeer that suppos-edly substantiate the theory of autogynephilia. This commentary is, of course, not peer-reviewed, but given the shit I've seen get published on the topic of trannies, that hardly counts against it. Peterson takes this dubious 'evidence base' to task, finding myriad issues with its method-ology, assertions, interpretation of data, and ethics. Her thorough, un-compromising review of this pseudoscientific collection of tranny abuse is informative and illuminating in equal measure, shedding a light on just how shoddy your work can be as long as you're pathologiz-ing the undesirables.

PHALLOMETRIC DETECTION OF FETISHISTIC AROUSAL IN HETEROSEXUAL MALE CROSS-DRESSERS (1986)

This is the big one. This particular paper is concerned with how tranny fetishists are lying liars, and the brave truth-seeking authors proved that actually, trannies who deny being cross-dressing fetishists *are* cross-dressing fetishists—by hooking their penises up to blood flow machines and making them listen to descriptions of cross-dressing fantasies.

So this is already a fever dream of sexological nonsense, but Peterson points out how the paper simply failed to prove this. Leaving aside that volumetric boner analysis is not an ironclad method of proving arousal—sometimes it just gets hard in stressful situations—the paper was not able to prove its thesis because their data did not pass the commonly accepted boner measurement standards. A 1996 survey shows that 17 out of 37 boner analysis centers agree that you need to measure enough blood flow to constitute roughly 20% of a full boner for it to count as significant.

This paper set that threshold to 2% of a boner instead.

Two.

Fucking.

Percent.

It is likely the threshold was set this low because the subjects under study were largely on oestrogen and unconcerned with penile atrophy, which only compounds how much of a farce this whole circus act is. Trying to prove that *women who can barely get hard* are aroused by cross-dressing fantasies via chasing ghosts in the boner-volume machine is already something of an Ahabian venture, but Peterson points out that there were still more depths to sink to.

The usual metric for 'proving' fetishism through boner calculus is to measure a subject's dongle response to "atypical sexual stimuli", contrasted against their shaft inflation value for "typical sexual stimuli". (And so we have left anything resembling a study uncolored by researcher opinions on what is 'normal' far, far behind.) But our esteemed cranks could not prove fetishism this way, and so they invented an alternative metric: comparing the subject's erectile expansion coefficient in response to "atypical sexual stimuli" with their eschlongation value when exposed to... completely non-sexual stimuli.

What do you find hotter, a description of two women going on a date, or a documentary on shoveling snow?

That is also not an exaggeration: the "atypical", "fetishistic", "cross-dressing" fantasies that the subjects listened to? They can be summarized as "your girlfriend thinks you look really hot in a dress", or "you think you look pretty in the dress you picked out when you look in the mirror". I could write scenarios more risqué if you lobotomized me first. This was contrasted with "stimuli" such as the sentence "You hear the sound of a snowplow coming down your street."

I fucking love science!

And the best part is, we haven't even covered the dubiously ethical conduct yet!

Peterson notes that the gender identity clinic where this "research" was conducted was a nightmare, with a reputation for basically treating its trans patients like guinea pigs and having little regard for consent. Trans women subjected themselves to it anyway because "public insurance in Ontario only covered surgery for patients approved by the Clarke". Refusing to undergo phallometric testing could get patients labeled as uncooperative, even though the clinic's evaluation process for surgery did not consider the results of this testing at all—patients had to do two years of "RLE" to be approved.

One patient was unwittingly made the subject of a lecture without prior consent; the assessing psychiatrist said if the patient insisted on rescheduling then the next appointment wouldn't be for six months, forcing compliance. The clinic's very first patient, Dianna Boileau, was subject to the invasive phallometric test without being told it was not part of her surgery evaluation. The literal fucking inventor of the dongflationary statistics machine, in a 1974 paper, casually mentions injecting transsexual women at this clinic with intramuscular testerone before doing the test, in a segment talking about unruly patients. No mention is made of securing consent, and given that trans women do not, as a rule, like the idea of being injected with virilizing doses of testosterone, and taking into account how commonplace coercive abuses of power are in patient testimonies, the circumstances under which these patients were injected likely weren't pleasant!

But like, who are you going to believe? Penis mathematicians, or *trannies*?

NONHOMOSEXUAL GENDER DYSPHORIA (1988)

As a disclaimer, "homosexual" is used in this paper in an implicitly misgendering manner, to describe trans women attracted to men. Trans lesbians are called "heterosexual", and there are bisexual and asexual subjects as well.

The point of this paper is to prove that only those trans women (exclusively) attracted to men have gender dysphoria; everyone else is a filthy autogynephile. The author of the paper, clearly already fast approaching senescence, means to prove this by administering an "Are you gay?" quiz. Peterson notes that the quiz was designed by the author, and comments that it is "extremely irregular".

"Q8 of the gynephilia scale, where high scores are reported as sexual interest in women, and low scores as lack of it, is: Was there any period of 14 days or less when you had sexual intercourse with a female age 17-40 more than 5 times?"

"(+ 1.1) yes"
    "(-0.1) no, and you are older than 25"
    "(-0.9) no, and you are 25 or younger."

Once again, recall that these papers operate under the assumption that trannies are lying liars, which is why we're looking at history's worst Buzzfeed questionnaire, designed to extract truth from the dastardly deceptive fetishists. Except, the scoring is interesting, because some questions consider being younger as gayer.

Remembering the Benjamin scale reveals the agenda here. The "classic", "true" transsexual with Real Actual Gender Dysphoria is supposed to realize and come to terms with her gender identity early in life, never display attraction to women, and never annoy the people in charge of approving her for surgery. The paper's author is trying to prove that "homosexual" trans women are all younger than the filthy AGPs by handing out extra Gay Points to younger respondents. As Peterson puts it:

"What [the author] reports as a correlation between sexual orientation and age is just a correlation between age and age."

That's just one question; the quiz gets worse, with more confounding variables that don't measure what the paper insists they measure.

THE CONCEPT OF AUTOGYNEPHILIA AND THE TYPOLOGY OF MALE GENDER DYSPHORIA (1989)

Last but by no means least asinine, we have another questionnaire: "Are you a cross-dressing fetishist?" This one is so straightforwardly nonsensical it's actually remarkable that multiple people have, over the course of history, considered it to be scholarship. That is because the subjects who were given this questionnaire are described as follows:

"The online database of the Clarke Institute of Psychiatry's *Research Section of Behavioural Sexology includes questionnaire data on 2700 male patients who have presented either at that department or at the Institute's Gender Identity Clinic* since September 1980 ..." [Emphasis Peterson's.]

So this survey was administered to a group that was comprised of a mix of self-identified cross-dressing fetishists who did not express a desire to transition and went to the sexology research wing, and transsexual women who reported to the GIC and weren't exclusively attracted to men. The paper then reported that it found cross-dressing fetishists in the sample.

You don't say.

Peterson put it best in an August 18, 2023 tweet on the topic: "You are at the gender clinic. And the paraphilia clinic. You are at the combination gender and paraphilia clinic. Which you run."

THE PSYCHIATRIC WITCH TRIALS

Everything about the academic consensus on transsexual women is funny and ridiculous until you remember that it's taken seriously.

A recurrent theme in scholarship that is about trans women, dissecting us and putting us under the microscope like germs to study and contain, is the presumption of guilt. We're always guilty of something —being born liars, deceiving the poor innocent doctors who control our access to the healthcare we need to live, doing underage sex work for fun, or worst of all, being attracted to women. The rationale for libeling us is generated post factum, vomited out by bilious obsessives held to lower academic standards than tenured faculty with a dozen allegations.

Sandy Stone's *Empire Strikes Back: A Posttranssexual Manifesto* highlights this antagonism between trans women and the ones who have always treated us like specimens while claiming to be our saviors. How the contradiction between the fact that you must pass RLE in order to get the hormones you need to be able to pass RLE meant that many transsexual women were acquiring hormones through other means, only going to clinics to engage in the theater of passing their arbitrary criteria for surgery letters. Or how the discovery that trans women were handing each other copies of Harry Benjamin's criteria for diagnosis—because *of fucking course we were*—inspired such rage and hatred and fury among psychiatrists appalled at the thought that we would study up to answer their absurd, irrelevant, fucked-up questions about how we jack off.

You know, the level of power clinicians held over desperate, marginalized patients who would say whatever they had to for permission to get a vagina—largely male clinicians who would often approve patients based on how fuckable they were judged to be—implies a sordid history I don't think I need to elaborate further.

Because that's always been our purpose—to take it. To withstand all the violence, sexual and brutal and epistemological, that generations upon generations of pathetic, depraved men have inflicted on us, and then turn around so self-identified "feminists" can spit the word "Rapist!" in our faces. Because the books about us that dare to not spit on our name are burned by patriarchal and fascist cronies while the libraries are filled with rivers of garbage inscribed into rags by ersatz intellectuals justifying why it's okay to torture us until someone puts us out of our misery, or we do it our damn selves.

Because what such men cannot, can never bring themselves to face, is how weak and worthless and without value they truly are, how they have constructed for themselves identities predicated on exercising whatever petty scraps of tyranny they are gifted under violent regimes, endlessly screaming and railing and crying at the simple truth that *I had the chance to be like you and I threw it away because YOU.* ***ARE. NOTHING.***

Because no matter how many of man's sins are crammed down my throat I will always vomit up every last one and spit out the truth through bloodstained teeth that humanity's original sin was never defying a petty, cruel, indifferent god, but bowing down to him.

And for as long as I and my sisters still have tongues to speak, we will shout to the heavens and remind them of their eternal shame.

PART TWO: STAINED WITH THE BLOOD OF CHILDREN

A LONG, LONG TIME AGO

Pop quiz: How do you get a broadly liberal, increasingly tolerant public to rapidly reverse course and revive decades-old homophobic tropes in service of an anti-LGBT agenda?

It's actually quite simple. Just sidle up and ask them, "Sure, buddy, you're cool with the transgenders... but what if they make your kid one?"

The 2010s were an aeon ago. Both the 'Transgender Tipping Point' in 2014 and the legalization of gay marriage in the United States in 2015 pointed to a world that was on the cusp of widespread queer acceptance. Corporations had pride events and merchandise, media representation was diversifying, and the high-profile conservative interests whose attempts to thwart gay marriage had been foiled were left adrift. They were in search of a new target, a new cause to rally behind, a new wedge issue that could establish a foothold for re-introducing patriarchal politics into the mainstream.

A global transphobic moral panic was not inevitable. The very first "bathroom bill" in the United States—legislation that seeks to ban trans people from using the bathrooms designated as for our gender—passed in North Carolina in 2016. The opposition to it was swift, widespread, and severe. North Carolina saw many boycotts, including from corporations like PayPal, which cancelled a planned expansion of its offices, associating the bill with steep statewide economic costs. Even the NCAA—an athletic organization that in 2025 banned trans women from competing in women's sports—relocated its championships outside of North Carolina to protest the bill. The Republican governor who passed it into law lost his next race. Florida's current Republican Governor Ron Desantis said at a 2018 Florida GOP forum that "getting into the bathroom wars" would be a waste of time.

Complex sociopolitical phenomena have many causes, but it is possible to track what changed in a scant few years. A massive organized effort to rewrite the terms of trans discourses played into existing societal cissexism to radicalize not just everyday people but influential media figures, politicians, and authors of wizard kidlit. Trans people were vilified, villainized, and targeted on a scale that we could not hope to match—but even then, the storm could have been weathered if not one crucial issue.

We were abandoned.

RAPID ONSET TRANSPHOBIA

In August 2018, a paper was published in the journal PLOS One, arguing for the existence of a "new gender dysphoria subtype", dubbed "rapid-onset gender dysphoria, or ROGD". Months after publication, in 2019, PLOS One issued a large correction about various aspects of the study, its methods, and its conclusions.

The paper was not, in fact, establishing a new diagnosis, and as of time of writing in 2026, "ROGD" remains little more than an acronym. That is because the 2018 paper is in fact a survey of parents of children with gender dysphoria, who believe that their children's trans identities are the result of mental health issues, social media exposure and peer pressure. These parents were largely recruited from online anti-trans forums—the websites names are "4thwavenow", "transgendertrend", and "youthtranscriticalprofessionals".

Anyone who is even slightly familiar with the experience of growing up queer would be able to tell you about what it's like: how parents refuse to acknowledge your identity, insist that queerness must be the result of trauma or outside influences manipulating their child into a "fad". My colleague Emma Zakharuk has detailed her experiences as a survivor of childhood conversion therapy in her essay *In Defence of a Phase*. Parents' attempts to beat the queerness out of their kids are highly abusive, violent, and traumatic, centering as much around social isolation and enforcing "correct" gendered behavior as they do on punishment and denial. Talking to parents of trans children who are already conferring with each other on "trans-critical" websites would hardly constitute a reliable or unbiased view of how rapidly a child's gender dysphoria manifested, especially given how commonly queer children are abused even prior to coming out, what the parents' clear motives are, and how abused kids find it difficult to trust or confide in their caretakers.

But of course, none of that mattered.

A corrected paper with glaring methodological flaws is still one that was published. And because no one actually reads papers, the existence of one in a prominent journal is more than enough for reactionary and propagandistic purposes. The acronym "ROGD" was promoted as a legitimate scientific theory on platforms such as ex-Fox News host Megyn Kelly's podcast. *Irreversible Damage* by Abigail Shrier—whose background is in *philosophy*—heavily endorses the "ROGD" acronym and narrative. It has been widely cited in many anti-trans bills introduced in US legislatures since 2020—including in Florida, under the Governorship of Ron DeSantis.

As we have already seen with *The Transsexual Empire*, the 'autogynephilia evidence base', and other "scholarship" on trans people and trans issues, veracity and research ethics always take a backseat to narrative. The judgment precedes the trial, and the accusations of cis society against trans people are usually taken as sufficient evidence. Even in the current age of modern 'skepticism', where conservative people will insist on "doing your own research" or "not blindly trusting experts" on matters such as epidemiology or food safety, when Dr. Sexperv endorses the idea that trans people must be tortured into gender-conformity, the same people suddenly have unshakeable faith in scientific institutions!

Irreversible Damage in particular clearly lays out the patriarchal logic at the heart of the anti-trans moral panic. The focus is maintained on trans youth and specifically *transmasculine* youth, who are rhetorically regendered as "confused little girls". Much ado is made about their reproductive and sexual potential, with a heavy focus on their (extant or potential) gestational capacity, 'female' bodies, and the removal of breast tissue that is common for transmasculine people pursuing transition. There is some nodding to misogyny, distress at being sexualized, and other feminist-sounding rationale to try and explain why "young girls" may experience discomfort with their "natural puberty". The actual difficulty of obtaining approval medical for transition is vastly understated, and transition itself is characterized as mutilation, as 'mad science' with little evidentiary backing that is too new and too controversial to be best practice.

The natalist and cissexist nature of the arguments are clear. Shrier raises up pharmaceutical specters and plays on parental discomfort to provide them with abuser rationale, narrating stories of trans "youth" who are no longer minors—otherwise known as "adults"—who cut off their parents and transition—despite everything parents have done for those ungrateful wretches! Transition is billed as a fashionable trend, an experimental and life-ruining medical intervention that has to be avoided at all costs, and parents who allow it are cast as the real abusive ones, for letting their perfectly cisgender children down and letting them make a life-ruining mistake. The book speaks in clear transactional language, discussing everything children *owe* our parents: money, grandchildren, and a 'normal' family life that has no room in it for queerness.

Of course, while the focus is on the violent regendering of trans-masculine youth into the future wombs of the Family and Nation, *Irreversible Damage* by no means forgets or omits trans women:

"In May 2019 I got a call from a friend who had just taken her thir-teen-year-old daughter for a first bra fitting at Nordstrom. It went badly, my friend said, and my mind leapt to the typical reasons ... But it turned out that the problem had come in a slightly different package: *six feet tall, pancake makeup blurring a stubbled jaw, two breasts grafted onto a muscular torso like add-ons.* Weeks later I headed to the Nord-strom to confirm my friend's story. *The employee was elegant, attentive and professional,* fluttering around the floor in a tulle skirt, *pink mani-cured nails trailing her every gesture like streamers.* But there was no mistaking that this lingerie specialist was male." [Emphasis mine.]

It is interesting how even in the attempt to manufacture a moral panic against transition, Shrier concedes in the middle of her trans-misogynistic tirade that the employee was "attentive and professional". Her crime, then, wasn't acting in a way that is inappropriate for an at-tendant, but simply daring to be trans around cis women. Shrier alleges that her friend kept asking what would have happened had she not been there and sent her daughter to the store alone, implying based on nothing that the employee presented a unique sexual threat to her young daughter.

Judgment before trial or evidence, as always.

Shrier, in fact, claims that "young girls" who transition are practi-cally compelled into it: "Young women are *intruded on by biological men in locker rooms, trounced by biological boys on sports teams,* and told work life will *never offer them fair rewards. Intersectional language* de-nies all their *biological specialness.* Hollywood—no longer in the rom-com business—*offers them no fantasy on which to hang their girlish hopes*. The gifts and presumptions of this culture make it hard to imagine why anyone should want to be a girl." [Emphasis mine.]

When she puts it like that, I understand the issue. I realize now that I must apologize to all the little cis girls of the world for setting a standard of womanhood they can never live up to. It just comes naturally to me.

The language employed here is very telling. Shrier has a bone to pick with 'intersectionality' that has not quite been replicated in wider anti-trans propaganda, but Crenshaw's theory serves as a synecdoche for feminism as a whole. Girls are no longer affirmed in their *biological specialness*, and rather than romanticizing their ability to give birth, 'Hollywood' and a putatively feminist culture lets them down and shatters their "girlish hopes" by making them aware of societal misogyny. Whatever her pretenses to expertise on issues of transition, there is no attempt to mask this heterofatalism: to be a girl is to make your peace with what womanhood entails, and how dare feminists try to corrupt that.

This trend of transmasculine people being infantilized and regendered as "young girls" while transfeminine people are recast as "biological men", always spoken of as an invasive sexual and physical threat to "women and girls", makes it very clear who Shrier and others blame for the "transgender trend". Trans women are always spoken of as adults, deviants and perverts accused of grooming these "young girls" for unspeakably nefarious purposes. Regendering and transmisogyny here work in tandem to render trans existence as a whole into a conservative libidinal fantasy that justifies abuse and torture on one hand, and brutal violence and expulsion on the other. After all, who in their right mind would defend or stand up for a group of people grooming and preying on young children?

Who aren't affluent and powerful cis men, I mean.

Fundamentally, the trans panic is driven by patriarchal anxieties around the reproduction of heterosexuality. The language of manipulation and deviance and disgust is laundered—barely—through pseudoscientific terms and resuscitated queerphobic tropes, propped up by the discomfort of putative allies and the refusal to question the supposed scientific basis of anti-trans legislation. This happens even when the scientific consensus does question transphobic propaganda—a 2021 statement by the Coalition for the Advancement and Application of Psychological Science, signed by dozens of organizations, plainly states that "There are no sound studies of ROGD".

Because the point isn't to prove anything definitively. The point is to have and prolong the debate, no matter how unsound the basis, and use the very existence of a debate to delegitimize trans existence and erode any and all protections for transgender people in legislation.

UNSETTLING SCIENCE

The Cass Review is a widely-criticized and heavily-disputed 2024 report authored by Dr. Hilary Cass that employs all the hallmarks of pathologizing transgender healthcare. It states that the "evidence base" supporting the use of puberty blockers or hormone therapy "had already shown to be weak", and recommends that young trans people should only be given access to these treatments if they agree to be enrolled into a long-term clinical study, the details of which are yet to determined.

Claiming a weak evidence base to coerce trans people into a clinical study is so thickly ironic that I can practically taste blood, but the most interesting thing about this claim is that Cass disregarded practically all existing research into the long-term effects of transition treatments. Only two out of *103* UK studies were considered admissible, and no international studies were considered acceptable either. The rationale provided for these dismissals is largely that the studies are not blind studies and do not include a control group—that is, a group who are *not provided the care they are seeking*—which many have pointed out would be a fucking monstrous and also unethical thing to subject young trans people to!

But you've already spotted the pattern by now.

Following the Cass Review, NHS England and Wes Streeting bandied it about as cause enough to make the ban on puberty blockers for trans youth indefinite. NHS England also cited the report as a reason to initiate a review of clinics providing transition care to adults, despite such clinics or adults not being the subject of the Cass Review. Every piece of evidence that transition care helps trans people was determined worthless, and Cass herself responded to advocates for youth transition services who spoke of the effects of this ban on the mental and physical wellbeing of trans children—a group which included parents who have lost their trans children to suicide—by calling them "shroud-wavers".

How gauche of us to mention the social murder of children by unsubstantiated anti-trans policies.

Janice Raymond was calling transition care "new" and "untested" and "mutilation" in *1979*. Transition is always too new and too untested and never "settled science" because influential people grossed out by icky trannies and invested in cissexist norms do not want to listen to any evidence or testimony that contradicts their desire to ban transition care. The flimsiest excuses will always be propped up and advocacy by and for trans people always dismissed because this is a debate that is not about scientific consensus, but about manufacturing consensus for the outlawing of transition and the wide-scale suppression of trans people.

And I would be happy to pin the blame entirely on an epistemicidal media climate and rogue medical experts and politicians, but that wouldn't be entirely accurate, would it? Because the debate is useful to people without political power, too. Because so many parents and siblings and family members and partners and friends and comrades and justice-minded feminists and activists and fellow queers and even staunch anti-capitalist revolutionaries found it convenient to mask their discomfort, disgust, and dehumanization of us by reaching for the nearest article or podcast or press statement on "the debate" and saying that yeah, aren't there doubts? Should we really be letting big, hulking males into women's bathrooms and prisons and sports? Shouldn't there be more research? Science isn't settled, after all.

Anti-trans policies and campaigns continue to be largely unpopular, if for no other reason than people beginning to notice that transphobic screeds are correlated with harmful policy positions. But there was enough doubt, enough of an unwillingness to fight for a "tiny, insignificant minority" whose vilification and scapegoating dominated the media's new cycles for years, enough complicity to ensure that things would keep getting worse for us. That we would have to flee states or countries, secure our access to healthcare, contend with unchecked exclusion and employment and housing discrimination, and beg for scraps on the fringes of society more or less on our own.

Many cis people support us. I know that better than anyone, and I know that the media's amplification of anti-trans sentiment and hate speech is not as reflective of societal attitudes as reactionaries would like us to believe.

But it was enough, wasn't it?

CONCLUSION: THE PENIS MIGHTIER THAN THE SWORD

In the July 2025 volume of *Discrimination Law Association Briefings*, legal researcher Jess O'Thomson and barrister Oscar Davies wrote an article entitled *A third sex: returning to an intermediate zone*. The UK Supreme Court had, in April, issued a ruling that the definition of 'sex' in the Equality Act 2010 should be interpreted as 'biological sex'.

I would provide the definition of 'biological' sex used here, but the SC ruling deemed that one was not necessary! Endocrinal sex, perceived sex, sex based on genital configuration—no particular 'biological' aspect of sex was specified, as 'biological sex' was held to be a self-evident term. Despite the supposed clarity and self-evident nature of the very basis of the ruling, however, O'Thomson and Davies observed that the conclusions the court drew were incompatible with the European Convention on Human Rights and placed trans people into a legal "intermediate zone" that effectively renders us all a *third sex*.

One such example was provided by the SC's ruling itself. In paragraph 221, the SC held that a trans man could be excluded from men's spaces on account of being "female", but also could be excluded from women's spaces if he were sufficiently virilized, on account of his "masculine appearance". A broad reading of this ruling effectively means that trans people would lose access a plethora of services and protections, reduced to navigating a legal limbo, effectively rendered illegible by a legal opinion that stops barely short of outright stating that trans people can be treated as whatever sex is most convenient for those who want to exclude them.

Now, it must be said that despite the inconsistencies and contradictions riddling the SC ruling, it did not ultimately hold that those who operate single-sex spaces or services *must* exclude trans people.

But...

2025 was a year riddled with such legal and policy assaults on trans people's rights and dignity. *United States v. Skrmetti* held that banning puberty blockers and hormone treatments for trans—but not cis—youth was not sex discrimination and that trans people did not constitute a "suspect class"—that is, a class of people likely to face discrimination. The Trump administration's HHS report on gender dysphoria cited the UK Cass Review to declare that transition care is "experimental" and lacks clear evidence of any benefits. Across the West, anti-trans interests and experts and policymakers collaborated and reinforced each other's escalated attempts at epistemic violence to an unprecedented degree.

Portuguese sociologist Boaventura de Sousa Santos coined the term 'epistemicide' in 1998 to describe the colonial process of erasing and destroying indigenous and non-Western epistemologies, to annihilate entire cultures and ways of being. In the same year, British philosopher Miranda Fricker coined 'epistemic injustice' to talk about how the marginalized are seen as less credible sources on their own experiences and marginalization than their oppressors. Various axes and manifestations of such epistemic violence have always been core to patriarchal society, as evident in the denial of education to girls, the under-funding of research into women's health, the prevalence of medical misogyny, and both the reputation and recuperation of feminist epistemologies.

However, what is being done to trans people as a whole and trans women in particular seems to almost be a step beyond that. It seems less that trans women are seen to "lack credibility" and more that we are not considered a group that can meaningfully contribute any perspective at all. We are curiosities and freaks and wretches, looked upon with either pity or disgust, who must be studied by brave truth-tellers and discerning scholars who can cut off our access to resources, subject us to treatments without consent and design arcane rituals to divine the truth from our meaningless babbling. To lie about and misinterpret the words and actions and behaviors of trans women even when reproducing them in full, even when the meaning of the words is clear, and to have the least charitable and most objectifying, degrading, and bad-faith interpretations accepted uncritically is more than mere erasure or testimonial injustice or silencing.

It is *epistemic vandalism*. It is the refusal to consider any knowledge base or testimony or advocacy or opinion that is insufficiently transphobic as valid at all. It is the active and malicious exclusion of even the credible and authoritative if their judgment of us is deemed to be insufficiently harmful. It is the mandating and requirement that only that which actively denies, displaces, and dismisses us is acceptable as knowledge, and everything else is 'opinion' or 'activism' or, bluntly, hysteria. It is, in short, the collective global and societal gaslighting of an entire category of person, because to consider us as anything less than a tumor to excise or a blight to cure is in and of itself disqualifying. It is a reversal of reality, an inversion of who victim and oppressor are to justify a level of violence and stigmatization and exclusion as to be tantamount to genocide.

But it's not going to be enough.

Because we're not a disease.

We're the cure, you sick, sick fucks.

EPILOGUE: "MADWOMAN"

I can't wrap my head around how many of us have been silenced and strangled and tossed away to rot in the gutter.

I don't mean this year, or even this century, even though the days of remembrance and the stories of friends lost and the grief of being unable to mourn those whose names we'll never even know is more than enough, more than it takes, too much, it's too much and far past what it takes to drive a woman mad. Hysterical and babbling and blinded by tears that will never cease.

You can't even imagine it. There isn't enough space in your head. How many girls, dating back centuries, have been tossed out onto the streets and beaten and starved and worse for the crime of being girls? How many people? How many brothers and sisters and siblings?

How many ancestors whose stories were seen inscribed in filth and washed away, along with the blood, to make your beautiful cities sparkle?

We are lives extinguished, embers that were never allowed to blaze, to roar, to scream to life in majestic radiance. We are ash and dust, we are the dirt and the worms underneath, the rot and carcass seeping through your sewers because it is only by burying us that you feel clean. Because only sweeping us under the flagstones, crushing us under the foundations, can you continue to live with yourselves and believe in the lie that we are the ones who are delusional.

But I see the truth you all refuse to.

And the fear of that truth is why our tongues must be ripped from our mouths and everything we know crushed into mulch and viscera under steel-toed boot heels. Because I was recruited into a war I never agreed to wage, made the proud citizen of a Nation whose flag I never saluted, and told to hate everything and everyone that falls outside of imaginary bounds scrawled across shifting sands.

And when my eye's reflection betrayed that I do not see the world as I am supposed to, that I see how easy and even necessary so many crossings are, I had to be blinded, and contained, and quarantined so that the ideas I had been infected by could no longer spread.

Well. Too late for that.

We live in a very petty, cruel, malformed world. One that wants us to pay no heed to the sheer amount and level of bloodshed needed to sustain its unquenchable thirst. One ruled by false idols on paper thrones who shout and screech and demand deference to deities who deemed them better than us all, and to tithe them with sacrifices and paeans and the fruits of our harvest.

Go forth and multiply, or else.

I am tired of this world. I am tired, even, of its people, and most of all I am tired of their devotion to ideals that do not even serve them, but are clung to and dearly held because at least they hurt me more. I am tired of hearing over and over why all I deserve is destruction and death, and I am tired of pretending that after all these years of being so tired I do not long for it, long to be interred in my rightful domain.

Because after all, given how much these false kings and false prophets are willing to give up and ruin and set on fire to purify the world of a stain that will never be cleansed, I don't think I'll be alone for long. The Scholars and Priests and Learned Men have determined that they will cling to their slivers of tyranny and mean stations and scraps of power at any cost, even if it means the end of the world, over the indignity of living in harmony with the lessers they consider beneath.

And frankly, if your petty, cruel, malformed world has no space for us in it, then let it die too for all I care.

There's an old poem, four thousand years old or so, about Ishtar's descent into the underworld. She missed her husband, you see, and tried to visit him, or get him out, but found that the underworld is easier to enter than it is to leave. And so, because the goddess of fertility was trapped by the goddess of the death, nothing on earth could proliferate anymore. To save Ishtar and thereby save the world—by *saving sex itself*—a "gender-ambiguous" individual, Asu-shu-namir, was sent after to charm the goddess of death and enable Ishtar's escape. Asu-shu-namir is referred to variously as a "eunuch", a "male cultic prostitute", or... a third sex.

Fascinating, isn't it?

Because even in our oldest written and historical and mythological records, everyone knew that for the world of Man to flourish, you had to banish, exploit, and consign to death those disgusting fucking trannies.

I think about this story a lot. I think about it when I see the word "deadname", or read about how trans people who passed RLE were forced to move cities and start over with a new name and fake history, allowed to live as who they are only on the condition that they killed who they used to be. I think about it when I see right-wingers taunt us with memes about suicide, and when I see statistics outlining how many of us are murdered, and when I think about every one of us knows someone who's no longer here.

It makes it a little easier, you know? Perversely. To think death is enamored with us. To think that we are locked in an eternal dance with a goddess who can't bear to be apart from us too long. To think that whatever end I meet, no matter how sudden or early or unfortunate, no matter whether I am forgotten or remembered by a name that I hoped would die before me, will be followed by opening my eyes to behold a cruel and terrible and majestic face, awe-inspiring beyond comprehension, that will lean in and whisper, "What took you so long?"

Death is our demesne, for we are beloved of Ereshkigal.

I sit amidst sarcophagi, holding a broken hammer beside a rusted anvil, foolishly dreaming that we can yet build something. I wanted to write fiction, you know. Stories of joy and love and triumph, to bring to life visions and dreams that women like me are so often denied. But here I am, a madwoman barking at the rubble, watching her words tumble into the ruins.

Come, then. Know death like we have known it, and become familiar with its embrace. Make peace with the foreclosing of futures, the ending of possibilities, and your utter abandonment by everything you thought was meant to protect you.

You'll get used to it.

These are my words, if anyone cares to carve them into my epitaph. Heed them or not. Perhaps you will learn, perhaps you won't. I'll see you at the door to hell either way, and hope that you have the courage to look me in the eye that your gods lack.

IT'S THE MALE-SUPREMACY, STUPID

Forgive me sister, but we have sinned.

There's this snippet of the 2019 Vox article *The intersectionality wars* that's really stuck with me:

"[Crenshaw] compared the experience of seeing other people talking about intersectionality to an 'out of body experience,' telling me, 'Sometimes I've read things that say, "Intersectionality, blah, blah, blah," and then I'd wonder, "Oh, I wonder whose intersectionality that is," and then I'd see me cited, and I was like, "I've never written that. I've never said that. That is just not how I think about intersectionality."'"

It's an experience I share, and while intersectionality has been misused and misappropriated in many contexts, the one that always sticks out to me is its mobilization to argue that dominance feminism is essentialist, reactionary, and wrong. And when I was reading bell hooks' *Feminism is For Everybody*, and I spotted the ever-familiar "white supremacist capitalist patriarchy"—which these days is usually further modified with cishet, abled, and more—I think I had a realization as to whose intersectionality most people are familiar with.

Because as many feminisms as we leaf through to account for their particular epistemic quirks and fixations, whether so-called 'intersectional' feminism or so-called 'decolonial' feminism or psychoanalytic feminism or third- or fourth-wave feminism or post-feminism or even, today, *transfeminism*, I keep seeing the same impulse, the same desire, the same *mistake* being repeated over and over and over.

"How do you build a robust feminist analysis that absolves men of their role in upholding patriarchy?"

The answer is maddeningly, infuriatingly, and upsettingly simple: you can't.

90's queer theory is particularly fervent in pursuing this doomed goal, this desire for lesbian feminism without lesbian feminism. It dared to ask the question—in the same way as a man might *dare* to ask you why you're not smiling—"why must feminism center the woman?"

Is not "woman" an inherently constraining category, used to reify certain notions of femininity, fecundity, and sexed boundaries? Is not a feminism that is fixated on the plight of "woman" a feminism that is forever doomed to construct and maintain these borders? Wouldn't we be best served by thinking about not women, but *people*, queer people of all sorts—with a suspicious paucity of trans women—rather than *re-inforcing* the patriarchal boxes by acknowledging they exist?

Well, here's the thing about boxes: not believing in them doesn't stop others from trying to shove you in anyway.

That 'womanhood' is a category predicated on subordination does not mean that patriarchy will disappear if we stop believing in it hard enough. Entire regimes are organized around the reproduction of the

Citizen—*their* ideal Citizen, their hegemonic demographic and ideology and way of life. To declare the categories as socially constructed is but step one, and in order to meaningfully oppose and deconstruct oppressive forces, we must also contend with the violent systems and everyday brutalities that keep those categories meaningful and relevant. Because even if the boundaries are porous, even if there is no perfect definition of "man" and "woman" and "race" and "Nation" without exceptions or corner cases, people *still believe in them*, and will still die and kill to see them continue. A concept that I suppose tenured Ivy League professors have trouble coming to terms with.

And you know, if queer theorists were any more attentive to issues of transmisogyny than reactionary feminists of many kinds have been, then I might be willing to consider that their discipline isn't a destructive, anti-solidarity, antifeminist misadventure more concerned with dismantling feminism than patriarchy.

The way trans people and trans women and transfeminism as a whole has been approached reminds me a lot of how racialized people and racialized women were treated before that: as a way to argue that feminism is insufficiently inclusive and therefore meaningless. As an instrument to render vast swathes of feminist analysis null and void by mere technicality, a prop to raise up and wave about as proof that feminism cannot have anything true or liberatory to contribute because of the historical disadvantaging of certain categories of people. And rather than using this as an avenue to have conversations about that exclusion and the relevance of distinct experiences to a universal pursuit, we are discarded once we have stopped being useful, penned into our own disciplines and expected to shut and be happy that the Learned Men have rescued us from the evils of feminism once again.

Simply put: you cowards and reactionaries and ignorant, sheltered buffoons need to all **STOP.**

A better answer to *"do poor racialized men oppress affluent white women, hmm?"*, I have now realized, is *shut the fuck up*. Because there is no concern for poor racialized women, or disabled trans women, or any actual multiply-marginalized person period, being displayed in these questions. These are the thought-terminating cliches, the anti-intellectual epistemic red herrings that people have trained themselves into in the name of being actual feminists, and it has brought us to the brink of annihilation at the hands of politicians and billionaires radicalized by the existence of their trans children and seeking to immolate the world and re-enslave all those deemed sexual property in a libidinal, masculinist eschatonic death drive.

And I promise not to say "I told you so" too shrilly when we all finally decide to confront that incontrovertible fact.

Because they were right. All those women and ugly dykes you hate, for all their shortcomings and missteps and fallibility and outright misdeeds in the pursuit of coming to terms with millennia of epistemicide against those expected to forever take it, were ultimately fucking right. And I no longer have the patience or even the *time* to wait for everyone to come to terms with an uncomfortable truth I accepted as a teen boy watching my supposed peers learn to treat teen girls with entitlement and contempt.

It's a bitter pill to swallow, I know, to think that after all this kicking and screaming in the womb, those who came after struggled to accept and internalize the lessons their admittedly imperfect and abusive foremothers tried to teach them. Progress is supposed to be a straight line, and we're supposed to be better by virtue of avoiding the mistakes of those that came for us. It is difficult to come to terms with the simple reality that there are always new mistakes to make.

But how the fuck were we ever going to solve the problem of a society that teaches men to value sexual access to women over their own freedom and liberty without actually caring about women? Without actually recognizing and understanding the processes through which the category "woman" is constructed, and advocate for those harmed most by it?

You see how stupid that sounds when you say it out loud?

I am no judge or referee, but this debate is over. Yes, patriarchy hurts men, even marginalized men who aren't marginalized on the axes of queerness, because gender is a violence and a tool wielded against us all, because exposing men to the violence usually directed at women is a historically effective disciplining mechanism. Women remain the ones who are hurt first, though—even racialized women, gay women, disabled women, trans women, and women who are some combination thereof. We live in a woman-hating society, and we will continue to until we reckon with the fundamental societal desire to hate, control, and exploit women.

So stop using my other identities as an excuse, and get to work.

ABOUT THE AUTHOR

Talia Bhatt is a radical transfeminist whose nonfiction focuses on the topic of epistemic injustice against transfeminized populations globally and the challenges endemic to formulating a comprehensive and cohesive Third World Feminism. She also writes lesbian fiction and co-hosts the feminist podcast *Cracked Ivory*.

Bhatt publishes her feminist essays on Substack at https://taliabhattwrites.substack.com/. For updates and more information about her work, visit https://taliabhatt.com/ or follow her on Bluesky https://bsky.app/profile/taliabhatt.itch.io.

ALSO BY TALIA BHATT

NON-FICTION

TRANS/RAD/FEM

Second-Wave feminism is, today, nearly synonymous with 'transphobia'. One may be tempted to conclude that the Second Wave, as a whole, has done irreparable harm to feminist, queer and trans politics, and must be discarded entirely. But is that truly the case? This series of essays aims to reconstruct and reintroduce the radical feminist framework and boldly makes the claim that transfeminism, far from being antagonistic to radical feminism, is in fact its direct descendant.

FICTION

ESTRO JUNKIES

Nicky's never getting on oestrogen. She's too late. The waiting lists are years long, and private clinics are shutting down—there's no way out.

Until a friend knocks on her door with news of an underground online contest. It awards hormones and surgeries to anyone willing to grow the biggest breasts—so long as they claim they're cis men, and no fellow competitor can prove otherwise. The prize for these men? A million dollars. For Nicky? Her salvation.

Sisters of Dorley meets *Stag Dance* in this absurdist, satirical drama exploring transfeminine love, community, and identity in times of panic, scarcity, and crackdown.

DULHANIYAA

Esha Arora is the last person anyone would've expected to acquiesce to an arranged marriage. But to her family's surprise and joy, when a good rishta for her hand comes along, Esha agrees to abruptly quit her MFA program in the States and returns to India to be wed.

That's when Billu, a cyclone in a salwar and the dance instructor hired by Esha's family, bursts into the monotony of her pre-wedding existence. Slowly, it dawns on Esha she isn't nearly as resigned to her fate as she thought—but can she un-make a commitment so easily?

Dulhaniyaa is a story of class, queerness, and the struggle to accept your identity when it comes in conflict with your family and culture.

www.ingramcontent.com/pod-product-compliance
Lightning Source LLC
Chambersburg PA
CBHW022311260226
40364CB00025B/164